Bible In Business Lens Expository

HOW TO START, SYSTEMIZE, AND SCALE YOUR BUSINESS WITH SCRIPTURE

DESHANTI GENUS

ALSO BY DE'SHANTI GENUS

Books Authored and Published

From Faith To Favor

Eagle, Find Your Voice

Eagle, Spread Your Wings

Other Books Published by Vizal

Monday Morning

Cook With Chef Decado

Bible
In
Business
Lens
Expository

© 2025 by De'Shanti Genus

Published by Vizal Publishing Services

Bridgeport, Connecticut

thepurposedeagle.com

Vizal Publishing is a Division of The Purposed Eagle Network.

Printed in the United States of America.

All rights reserved. No part of this publication may be reproduced, stored in a retrieval system, or transmitted in any form or by any means without the prior written permission of the publisher. The only exception is brief quotations in printed reviews.

Library of Congress Cataloging- in- Publication Data

Names: Genus, De'Shanti, author.

Identifiers: LCCN 2025912956 | ISBN | ISBN 9781734562255 (paper)

Subjects: LCSH: Bible. | Business. | Wealth.

Unless otherwise noted, Scripture quotations marked kjv are from the King James Version of the Bible. Scriptures marked niv are taken from the Holy Bible, New International Version®, NIV®. Copyright © 1973, 1978, 1984, 2011 by Biblica, Inc.® Used by permission of Zondervan. All rights reserved worldwide. www .zondervan .com. The "NIV" and "New International Version" are trademarks registered in the United States Patent and Trademark Office by Biblica, Inc.® Scripture quotations marked nlt are taken from the Holy Bible, New Living Translation, copyright © 1996, 2004, 2015 by Tyndale House Foundation. Used by permission of Tyndale House Publishers, Carol Stream, Illinois 60188. All rights reserved.

BIBLE IN BUSINESS LENS EXPOSITORY

Cover design by Vizal

Contents

Introduction	IX
START YOUR BUSINESS	XIV
1. God's Economy	1
2. David's Dynamic team	12
3. Move with Noah (Rest)	20
4. The FAT of Eglon: The Unconventional Advisor	25
5. Focus - Build The Wall	30
6. Solomon's Million Dollar Secret	44
7. Invest to Harvest	52
8. Gleaning and Mentorship	60
9. Little by Little	67
10. What's in Your Hand?	72
11. The Parable of the Talents	79
12. God's Divine Strategy	89

13.	Eating the Crumbs	97
14.	The Power of Leverage	102
15.	The Well	113
16.	The Lame Man- Get Your Power Back	123
17.	Stretch Your Tent - Cultivating The Growth Mindset	131
18.	The 9 Laws Of Giant Success	141
19.	The Journey, The Sojourner, and The Roadmap	160
20.	Vision Is The Anchor	168
21.	It's God's Business	176
22.	Don't trust AI (Achan's Intelligence)	183
23.	Systems!	192
24.	Conclusion	212
25.	About the Author	215
Notes		217

Introduction

Introduction

The very first verse of the bible frames the purpose of mankind and gives us insight into our origin, design, and destiny.

It is rich with revelation:

"In the beginning God created the heavens and the earth."

—Genesis 1:1, NLT

We are introduced to four divine keys:

God, created, heavens,
and
earth.

God created

. This is the first action we see from the God of the universe. Before He healed, ruled, judged, or even loved, He created. Creativity is God's opening act, and because we are made in His image, it is also a core part of who we are.

"Then God said, 'Let us make human beings in our image, to be like us. They will reign over the fish in the sea, the birds in the sky...'"

—Genesis 1:26, NLT

"Then the Lord God formed the man from the dust of the ground. He breathed the breath of life into the man's nostrils, and the man became a living person."

—Genesis 2:7, NLT

Here's what this is saying: you are a unique composite of both heaven and earth. Your body was formed from the earth (the Hebrew word adamah), and your spirit was infused with the very breath of God. You were born to operate as a heavenly solution in an earthly realm.

So what does that mean for you?

It means that you were made to create.

Creativity is not a random trait given to a select few. It is the image of God at work in every person. Whether you are an innovator, entrepreneur, artist, designer, strategist, or business builder—you are operating in your God-given nature when you create something that brings life, order, beauty, or value to others.

"For we are God's masterpiece. He has created us anew in Christ Jesus, so we can do the good things he planned for us long ago."

—Ephesians 2:10, NLT

You are not a mistake. You are not random. You are His masterpiece. You were made with intention, carrying both the soil of the earth and the breath of heaven. You were formed to bring forth good things; things that change lives, shape culture, and reflect God's glory on earth.

For the creatives, the builders, and the visionaries; this book is especially for you. It's for those who feel the tug to build something more--whether it's a business, brand, ministry, product, or platform. If you've ever felt that holy discomfort that says, "There is more in me to give," you're right

This book is your reminder that your creative instincts are not just a personality trait—they are a kingdom tool. Whether you are a CEO or a stay-at-home mom building something from scratch, the same Spirit who hovered over the deep in Genesis 1 is hovering over your life now, waiting for you to speak, build, and birth.

Welcome to *Bible in Business Lens Expository*; a book designed to explore timeless stories and principles from the Bible through the lens of business. This is not a theological text, nor is it meant to suggest doctrine or reinterpret

Scripture. The Bible stands complete in its meaning, and nothing in this book is intended to add to or take away from its truth.

Instead, my goal is simple: to draw out the wisdom embedded in Scripture and consider how it can be practically applied to the business world. Whether you're a startup founder, entrepreneur, or marketplace leader, this book offers a unique and inspiring way to connect your faith to your work.

Approximately two-thirds of the content is rooted in actionable, biblical principles that can influence how we build, lead, and grow businesses. The remaining third takes a creative look at biblical stories—using them as illustrative tools to spark thought and inspire business-minded reflection.

Let's explore how the ancient truths of Scripture can shape modern-day enterprise.

Ex footballer, Trent Shelton once said at an event, that when he left football to become an influencer, no one understood his dreams. He one day realized that God gave him his prescription glasses, and when he put them on, he could see crystal clear the man he was supposed to be. But when he gave others his glasses it was blurry for them. Simply put, your lens holds *YOUR* prescription. No one will be able to see out of your lens what you see. In entrepreneurship, it becomes a lonely road at times. The sad truth is that most times, it's not until you begin to see the fruit of your labor will people begin cheering for you. So in this book, I'm asking to pick up two pairs of lenses. The first, *your* prescription lens; the one that helps you see your future. The second--these business lenses that we will look at the bible through. Cheers to the success of your business.

START YOUR BUSINESS

1

God's Economy

I've seen enough—both in life and throughout the ages in Scripture—to be fully convinced that **God's economy** operates on a completely different system than the world's. One of the most personal and profound lessons I've had in this truth came in 2020.

My husband and I stepped into homeownership with just one consistent income—his job—and some savings. On paper, it didn't look like we had enough. But then, there was **God's economy**.

At the time, I had just been laid off, leaving me without a paycheck for nearly three months. And yet, during that period, I earned more personally than I would have if I had been working. How? A divine combination of God-given strategies and what I call the **supernatural provision of God's economy**.

I'll never forget one moment: I logged into a reserve bank account and saw over $1,000 sitting there. This was money I didn't have the day before—no invoices, no alerts, no explanations. It was as if God Himself had deposited a reminder that **He is my ultimate Provider**.

Meanwhile, my husband—ever wise and disciplined in finances—ensured we remained stable. As we searched for a home, we found a beautiful, modern Cape-style house that I instantly fell in love with. But it was at the very top of our budget. Our realtor advised us to move quickly because homes were flying off the market due to an influx of buyers relocating from New York to Connecticut. Hesitation could cost us.

Still, something didn't sit right. In the middle of that moment, I heard God whisper in my heart: **"I have something bigger in store for you."** Though I liked the house, I knew it wasn't *the* house. Disappointed but trusting, we walked away.

A few days later, while washing my hair, I came across Golda McFarlane's song *Bigger, Better* on YouTube. The lyrics struck me like lightning—it was confirmation. **God did have something greater planned.**

Sure enough, within weeks, the house we eventually bought reappeared on the market. The original buyer had lost their job and could no longer close. Not only that, but the asking price had dropped by $15,000—putting it *well* within our budget. In the middle of an economic downturn, when businesses were closing, **we stepped into a home that was significantly larger and better than the one we first considered**. To God be all the glory.

Two 24-year-olds bought a house during a global crisis.

How?

Two words: **God's economy.**

The keys? **Obedience. Faith. Trust.** Trusting that **God's provision isn't tied to worldly conditions**. When we operate within His economy, He provides in ways that defy logic.

Let's look at a powerful example from Scripture in **2 Kings 7**, where Elisha prophesies a radical economic shift:

Elisha replied, "Listen to this message from the Lord! This is what the Lord says: By this time tomorrow in the markets of Samaria, six quarts of choice flour will cost only one piece of silver, and twelve quarts of barley grain will cost only one piece of silver!" The officer assisting the king said to the man of God, "That couldn't happen even if the Lord opened the windows of heaven!" But Elisha replied, "You will see it happen with your own eyes, but you won't be able to eat any of it!"

—2 Kings 7:1–2 (NLT)

At the time, **Samaria was under siege by the Arameans**, and famine had devastated the land. It was so severe that people were buying donkey heads and dove droppings for food. The situation seemed utterly hopeless. Then came Elisha's bold declaration: **By tomorrow, there will be an abundance.** Given the state of the economy, this prophecy sounded laughable. One officer even said it couldn't happen "even if the Lord opened the windows of heaven." But Elisha responded that the man would see the miracle—but not partake in it.

If we rewind to **2 Kings 6**, the backdrop becomes clearer:

Some time later, however, King Ben-hadad of Aram mustered his entire army and besieged Samaria. As a result, there was a great famine in the city. The siege lasted so long that a donkey's head sold for eighty pieces of silver, and a cup of dove's dung sold for five pieces of silver. One day as the king of Israel was walking along the wall of the city, a woman called to him, "Please help me, my lord the king!" He answered, "If the Lord doesn't help you, what can I do?"

—2 Kings 6:24–27 (NLT)

Can you see how, naturally speaking, it would be difficult to believe that God could turn things around?

I think the greatest doubt wasn't just about *if* God could do it—but *how fast*. How could an economy so inflated—where people paid eight silver pieces for a donkey's head—shift to flour and barley being sold for just one piece of silver?

Yet that's exactly what happened.

The prophecy was fulfilled through **four lepers**, social outcasts, who decided to walk toward the enemy's camp. Unknown to them, **God had already caused the Arameans to flee**, creating the sound of a mighty army that terrified the enemy into abandoning their supplies. These lepers stumbled upon *abundance*—food, silver, clothing, and more. They reported it, and before long, the entire city had access to what they needed.

The officer who doubted? He was trampled at the gate—**he saw the blessing but never tasted it.**

This story teaches us a vital truth: **God's economy operates on faith, obedience, and divine timing**. It does not submit to natural circumstances. In this chapter and throughout the book, we will see Kairos time as a strategy God uses for businesses to grow. Kairos means: Moment of significance or an opportune time. It's a window in time that supersedes Kronos time; a "sudden" moment.

When Tenoy and I bought our home, these were the same principles that carried us through. I even remember the Lord telling us **when** to have the mortgage broker run our credit. In March 2020, when we first felt the nudge to start the process, God told us to wait. We obeyed and got pre-approved in April 2020—at exactly the right time.

He also led us to the **right mortgage broker**. She became a destiny helper. With her years of experience and deep industry network, she had a strong reputation. When we put in our offer, we weren't the only ones—but the seller's agent recognized our broker's name. Because of that, the seller chose **our offer**.

Two 24-year-olds, favored by the hand of God.

This is **God's economy** in action.

It doesn't run on the Dow Jones or job security. It runs on faith, divine timing, and a surrendered heart!

Many times, we look at our financial situations through the lens of worldly limitations—our income, market conditions, job security, or economic downturns—rather than seeing through the eyes of faith. The people in Samaria were starving because they were boxed in by their immediate circumstances, but God had already orchestrated their provision. That sentence deserves a big "SELAH" at the end of it.

The miracle wasn't about resources suddenly appearing; it was about a shift in perspective, availability, and obedience.

Similarly, in our lives, there are times when financial opportunities, promotions, or unexpected blessings are right within reach, but if we are not **spiritually sensitive to God's voice**, we might miss them.

I remember recently having a dream of being in an old school building. I was grown but still trying to take those classes that I kept missing. I was showing up late to the classes and trying to blame people for not prompting me to go. An angel met me in the dream in the form of a principal, to correct and redirect me. I know that this dream might be interpreted in many ways depending on who is reading it. However, God gave me an instant revelation of what it meant when I woke up. The devil's plan was to delay me in a specific myriad of events that were to happen. I should have "matriculated" through and been farther ahead in these things. God told me that I needed to have systems in place (which I'll talk about a little later in another chapter) and be extremely sensitive to His voice and timing. I've since been able to overcome those delays and successfully take on those events, thanks be to God!

Had the lepers been too fearful to move, they would have missed their role in God's supernatural breakthrough. Had the officer chosen to believe in God's word instead of mocking it, he could have enjoyed the provision instead of losing his life.

Faith is the currency of God's economy. I say this all the time! While the world's system is built on hard work, and supply-and-demand, God's system operates on trust, obedience, and divine strategies.

This is why we must **stay in tune with God's voice** when it comes to our finances. Many times, He will lead us to make unconventional decisions—whether it's starting a business in a recession, investing when it seems unreasonable, or sowing a financial seed when logic says to save. All three of these, I am too familiar with.

Those who lean on their own understanding may hesitate or even doubt, but those who trust God's voice will step into provision that doesn't make sense in the natural world.

The book of St. Matthew is another great book to see God's economy at work. Matt 16:6-11. Jesus forewarns the disciples to beware of the "leaven of the Pharisees." The disciples were disquieted because they actually left the real bread home. So they were thinking that Jesus was warning them about the bread they would have eaten from the Pharisees. Then Jesus clarifies in vs 8 what He was referring to.

Jesus knew what they were saying, so he said, "You have so little faith! Why are you arguing with each other about having no bread? Don't you understand even yet? Don't you remember the 5,000 I fed with five loaves, and the baskets of leftovers you picked up? Or the 4,000 I fed with seven loaves, and the large baskets of leftovers you picked up? Why can't you understand that I'm not talking about bread? So again I say, 'Beware of the yeast of the Pharisees and Sadducees.'"

-- Matthew 16:8-11 (NLT)

He was essentially saying to them " I already took care of the masses (5000), when we only had 5 loaves of bread and 2 fish. That could have **ONLY BEEN God's economy.**

In chapter17 of Matthew, Jesus was sitting with his disciples when the tax collectors came to take his payment. He simply told His disciples to go open the mouth of the fish and take out the money. The exact amount needed to pay the taxes **WERE IN THE MOUTH OF A FISH**!

I pray that in your business, you will begin to experience the divine economy of God. May your business shock others and lead them to Christ. My sincere hope is that this chapter has tugged on the faith strings of your heart. That you will receive everything else it has to offer.

God is not limited by recessions, job losses, or economic crises. Just as He turned Samaria's famine into abundance overnight, and just as He took money from the mouth of the fish, He can shift your financial situation in an instant. The key is being sensitive enough to hear His voice and bold enough to act when He speaks. The world's economy fluctuates, but **God's economy is always abundant for those who trust Him.**

2

David's Dynamic team

When British Billionaire Richard Branson (founder of Virgin Group) was asked the question, "what was one of the factors he attributes his success to", his answer was **building a strong team**. A famous quote of his is *"train people well enough so they can leave, treat them well enough so they don't want to."* That's a significant factor for building and maintaining a well established team. You can always build a great team with your skills, but if you don't make them feel appreciated and valued, then you won't see retention in your team. In a CNBC article published October 18th, 2017, by reporter Ruth Omuh wrote about Branson, *"traits that the entrepreneur looks for in his employees include being personable, detail-oriented and hardworking."*

Those traits are paramount for business growth. While those are amazing traits, I want to share a few more that another wealthy person looked for in his "team." This person was King David. We will begin to see what David's success was predicated on.

As you walk in your God-given purpose (especially as an entrepreneur) one truth becomes clear: *you cannot build something great alone.* Some entrepreneurs start solo, either by necessity or choice. But as the vision grows, so must the team. And not just any team, but *the right team*. A God-aligned team.

One Sunday morning during my quiet time, I opened my Bible and began reading Psalm 101. I didn't expect it to hit me the way it did. But the words of David pierced my heart.

David opens the psalm with a powerful personal commitment:

"I will be careful to live a blameless life—when will you come to help me? I will lead a life of integrity in my own home. I will refuse to look at anything vile and vulgar. I hate all who deal crookedly; I will have nothing to do with them."

—Psalm 101:2–3, NLT

These verses convicted me deeply. They reminded me that before I'm a businesswoman, coach, or visionary—I'm a **child of God**. My heart must remain submitted to Him. My motives must be aligned with His will.

Anyone I allow to come alongside me in business must carry that same standard.

The Leader's First Priority: The Heart

Before David starts correcting others, he examines *himself*. As a leader, this is vital. You can't demand integrity from others while neglecting your own heart. David says, "I will lead a life of integrity in my own home." In business terms: your character behind closed doors matters just as much as your public leadership.

Before building a team, *build your heart*. Your team will reflect your leadership. If there's disorder or hidden compromise in you, it will show up in your team. But if your heart is yielded and repentant, you'll naturally attract people who mirror that same purity, humility, and excellence.

What Kind of People Should You Avoid?

David doesn't just examine himself; he draws boundaries:

"I will reject perverse ideas and stay away from every evil. I will not tolerate people who slander their neighbors. I will not endure conceit and pride."

—Psalm 101:4–5, NLT

At first glance, we might assume David is just talking about "wicked" people. That seems obvious, right? But look again at what he identifies as wicked: **gossipers, slanderers, and the prideful.** Not just criminals or enemies; he's talking about people with destructive *attitudes*.

In business, these traits are toxic. You don't need people on your team who tear others down behind closed doors, or who carry inflated egos. You need those who uplift, protect, and walk humbly.

By the way, David isn't just making casual observations. He says, *"I will not endure them."* As in, *they will not be allowed in my space.* That's the posture of a surrendered and wise leader: someone who doesn't just protect the **vision**, but also the **culture** surrounding it.

A Warning from David's Story

One of David's trusted advisors, Ahithophel, was known for his incredible wisdom. The Bible even says:

"The advice Ahithophel gave was as though it had come directly from the mouth of God."

—2 Samuel 16:23, NLT

But Ahithophel eventually betrayed David, choosing to side with David's rebellious son Absalom in an attempt to overthrow him. His betrayal wasn't because of lack of wisdom, but because of a **misaligned heart**.

This proves something important: *intelligence, skill, and experience do not equal loyalty or divine alignment.* Don't be dazzled by someone's résumé. Be prayerful about their character. Ask God: *"Is this someone who belongs in my circle?"*

Who Should You Keep Close?

David doesn't just talk about who to avoid, no. He also tells us who to embrace:

"I will search for faithful people to be my companions. Only those who are above reproach will be allowed to serve me."

—Psalm 101:6, NLT

Notice, he doesn't say *"gifted"* or *"influential."* He says **faithful.**

Faithfulness is often overlooked in favor of talent. But I've learned through experience: you can train skill, but you can't manufacture loyalty. The person who shows up with consistency, who is teachable, who is committed to the vision even when it's not glamorous; that person is gold.

They may not fit the typical mold. They may not have a polished background. But if they're **faithful**, they can grow. And they'll grow *with* you.

Biblical Steps for Building Your Team Reviewed

1. **Do a Heart Check:** As a leader, visionary or CEO of your business, it is important to regularly evaluate your motives. Are you pursuing your purpose for God's glory or for personal gain? Invite God to purify your intentions.

2. **Build a Kingdom Team:** Look for people who share your values and are committed to excellence. Pray over your hiring decisions and trust God to bring the right individuals into your circle.

3. **Celebrate Small Wins:** Just like Branson said, you must make it a nonnegotiable to make your team feel appreciated. Celebrate their small wins. And be sure to celebrate yours. Make trackers for every project and every step needed to make business grow. Over time monitor and track your

increments of growth.

3

MOVE WITH NOAH (REST)

The Paradox of Building and Trusting God

At the end of the Jewish year 5784, I had a few significant moments where I knew the Lord was speaking to me about *movement*. One morning, on my way to work as a temporary dental hygienist, I was assigned to a dental office in Durham, Connecticut. As I pulled into the plaza, something immediately caught my eye. Right next to the office was a business called "Move with Noah."

At first, I didn't think much of it. But the phrase stayed with me. *Move with Noah.* That morning I decided to look up the meaning of the name *Noah*. To my surprise, it meant rest. *Move with Rest.*

It intrigued me, especially because a few days prior, I had come across the word *traverse* in a book I was reading.

The word piqued my curiosity because it had to do with movement; crossing through, navigating, going forward.

"Move with rest? How is that even possible" I thought to myself. It was a paradox; one that had deeper meaning than I realized at first. As mentioned before, we were coming to the end of one Jewish year and crossing over into the other one. So I knew prophetically and spiritually, I wasn't just entering into a new season, but into a new year. It felt different. And even though "movement" or transition means that things will change, God was reassuring me I would transition with rest. I was getting ready to enter a *"massive builders"* season that would demand a lot of attention. I would have to practice delayed gratification by missing out on events and experiences that would take away my focus.

Noah's Blueprint for Business and Life

The more I reflected on it, the more I realized that Noah's story held a powerful lesson I could learn from:

Delayed gratification leads to ultimate rest.

Noah had to build something no one had ever seen before. He had to construct an ark in preparation for rain that had never fallen. What a task of faith! While everyone else lived as if life would always continue the same way,

Noah worked. They laughed at him. They went on with their pleasures and their plans. But Noah kept building. He was *moving* through his season of building, but he had an unusual kind of *rest*.

Noah worked in obedience to God's vision, even when the results were not immediately visible. And that's the same mindset required in business. If you can build now, you can enjoy your rest later.

But even more than that, I believe Noah had a level of rest in the building process. It's not because it was easy, but because God was with him. He wasn't just moving; he was moving with God.

That's the key.

There's a supernatural peace that comes when you know that what you're building is aligned with God's purpose for your life.

What Are You Willing to Sacrifice to Build?

Noah sacrificed time, comfort, and social approval to complete his God-given assignment. And in business (or any major pursuit) you'll have to do the same.

So I ask you:

- What are you willing to give up now so you can experience rest later?

- What expenses can you cut to save?

- What distractions can you eliminate so your energy isn't wasted on things that don't serve your purpose?

- Who can you partner with to help build your vision?

Noah didn't build the ark alone. He had his family, his team. Likewise, success in business and in purpose requires community. You need the right people! You need the ones who believe in the vision, who can help carry the weight, and who will support you when the work gets hard.

Tenoy and I personally experienced this when God called us to build The Purposed Eagle Network. We were preparing for our second annual networking event and I was tired. We had a toddler, a newborn, and we were adjusting with new work schedules. But I couldn't shake the feeling that God wanted us to intentionally build this network and prepare for the event.

I remember one day crying out to God for help. He started to send the help we needed. He sent sponsors, and most importantly timely friendships. Friends that came and invested in the business and became core members even until this day. He laid it on someone's heart to sew a percentage of their earnings for 4 months into the business without us asking! What blessed me more was their testimony of God providing a $10,000 scholarship for their college after they obeyed him. My hope is that we see the power in moving with God. It may be uncomfortable at times, but always be assured that when God calls you to build something, you can trust that He will take care of you.

The Call to Build and Move with Rest

I believe God is calling many of us to build in faith. To work hard, but not in our own strength. To move with rest.

The world teaches hustle, grind, and exhaustion as the price of success. But the kingdom of God operates differently. There is a way to build and still remain in a place of peace. There is a way to work without fear, anxiety, or long periods of burnout. The answer?

Move with Noah. Move with rest. Move with God.

And just like Noah, you'll see the rain come. You'll see the doors open. When the floodwaters rise, you won't be swept away because you built on God's word.

4

THE FAT OF EGLON: THE UNCONVENTIONAL ADVISOR

One of the best pieces of advice I've received in the business world is that you need to listen to those who have experience in what you want to grow in. "Success leaves clues." There are people out there who have the answers to the questions we need. We just need to find them or ask God to send them. However, sometimes, these mentors won't look like who we expect. God will sometimes use people who are extremely different from us to plant a seed of knowledge that will propel us forward.

In 2024, while on maternity leave, I felt a strong tug to develop myself more in coaching. During this time, I specifically asked God to send someone who could help me with a method I was missing to elevate my program to the level I envisioned. There was someone I knew who had the knowledge I needed, yet I wrestled internally over whether listening to one of his free masterclasses or attending his three-day workshop was the right move. As I sought God's direction, He led me to a story in the Bible; one that, at first glance, seemed unrelated to business but carried an unconventional lesson I needed in that season.

The Story of Eglon and the Lesson of Extracting Knowledge

Eglon was a wicked king. He oppressed the Israelites daily. The Bible describes him as "very fat." No one was willing to fight him. Now, before we go any further, let me make this clear: the lesson I drew from this story is not its direct biblical context. However, I believe God allowed me to glean a valuable, unconventional insight from it.

Eglon was evil, but he was also "fat"—full of knowledge, resources, strategy, and power. Interestingly, the Hebrew meaning of Eglon is "bull." Biblically, bulls symbolize strength, wealth, power, and leadership. There are individuals in the world today who, though they may not walk in righteousness, still possess knowledge and principles that we can learn from.

This pattern is seen throughout Scripture. Daniel and the three Hebrew boys were trained in the language and customs of Babylon under a pagan king. Moses, though called to deliver Israel, was raised and educated in the Egyptian palace. Joseph, second in command after Pharaoh, had to learn the financial and administrative affairs of Egypt. These men remained steadfast in their faith while acquiring valuable knowledge from secular environments. Their learning did not compromise their devotion to God but rather equipped them for their divine assignments.

In Judges, we see that Ehud was the only one bold enough to confront and kill Eglon. How did he do it? He got close; close in proximity, close enough to strike. From this, I learned a powerful business lesson: sometimes, you must get close enough to extract the "fat" of the knowledge they carry. The goal isn't to stay in their systems or conform to their ways but to gain the wisdom necessary to move forward.

I want to make another disclaimer: this principle is not to be confused with seeking advice from witches, business intuitives, or any form of ungodly counsel. This is strictly about recognizing that some business strategies, leadership principles, and industry knowledge are universal. Just as you wouldn't question the faith of your college professor when learning a subject, you can learn from experienced individuals without it interfering with your spiritual life.

Applying This to Your Business Journey

As Christian entrepreneurs, we are called to grow our businesses God's way. However, that doesn't mean we ignore earthly wisdom that aligns with sound principles. The key is discernment; knowing what to take and what to leave. When God places knowledge in your path, even if it comes through an unlikely source, seek Him for wisdom on how to apply it.

The Bible says in Proverbs 4:7, "Wisdom is the principal thing; therefore get wisdom: and with all thy getting get understanding." If we want to build sustainable, impactful businesses, we must be willing to learn, even from those outside our immediate faith circles. Just as Ehud got close to Eglon to accomplish his mission, sometimes we must get close enough to gain the knowledge necessary to move to our next level. The key is remembering who we are, staying firm in our values, and using what we learn to glorify God in our work.

I remember another time recently being at work. One of my patients that day happened to be an entrepreneur for almost 3 decades. She was coming to the end of her career and was planning to retire. As we spoke, I asked her the question I ask most entrepreneurs: What is one piece of advice you would give to an aspiring entrepreneur. I'll never forget her answer. "BE YOUR BEST SELF. Because the greatest asset to your company is you!" She told me that what made her standout from all her peers in her industry was her ability to do things in excellence. She had a strong brand for consistency and professionalism. Towards the end of her appointment with me, she offered to give me more tips on a coffee meet up. Those were some of the best tips I had ever gotten from someone who walked the path of entrepreneurship. Were we from the same background? No. Did she have reliable resources I needed? Yes.

Reflection Questions:

1. Are there areas in your business where you need to seek guidance from someone more experienced, even if they don't share your faith?

2. How can you discern between knowledge that is beneficial and knowledge that contradicts your values?

3. What unconventional sources has God used in the past to give you insight and wisdom?

God is always working, and sometimes, His provision comes in unexpected ways. We will delve more into this point in the next chapter. Keep your eyes open, remain prayerful, and be willing to learn where He leads you.

5

Focus - Build The Wall

I must admit, this is the chapter that pushed me to complete this book. The principle here has been a core practice of mine for everything I do in entrepreneurship: writing books, planning events, creating courses, coaching, and posting content that serves others. This bible story fuels me whenever I am weak. It comes from an invaluable book: The book of Nehemiah.

It all begins with a problem. The walls of Jerusalem had been torn down. The gates were burned. There was no structure, no protection, no identity. God's people were left exposed and vulnerable. This news broke the heart of a man named Nehemiah, a Jewish man who held a prestigious position in the palace of Persia as the cupbearer to the king (Nehemiah 1:11).

Even though Nehemiah lived in comfort, he was not content. When he heard about the condition of Jerusalem, he wept (Nehemiah 1:4). He mourned, fasted, and prayed before the God of heaven. That's where vision was born.

God impregnated Nehemiah with purpose. This was the burden that shifted him from routine to assignment. The Bible says in Nehemiah 1:4, "When I heard these words, I sat down and wept. I mourned for a number of days, fasting and praying before the God of the heavens." What Nehemiah did next was remarkable: he didn't immediately act; instead, he waited on God. He remained burdened for months, praying earnestly. In fact, Scripture tells us he received the news in the month of Kislev (around November/December), but it wasn't until the month of Nisan (March/April) that he acted (Nehemiah 2:1). That's nearly four months of carrying the burden before the opportunity came.

This wasn't just a passing emotion, it was a true burden he carried and a true assignment.

At the end of 2023, when I was about eight months pregnant with my son, I, too, became burdened with another assignment. God began to stir something deep within me. I had a heavy burden for people who didn't know their purpose. I cried out to God, asking Him how I could help. That's when He gave me an answer: create an online course that would guide others in discovering and activating their God-given talents. Even though we hosted our "Purposed Eagle networking event" and I did videos online, I still felt like I needed to do more.

Here's the thing, I had never created a course before. I didn't even know where to begin. But just like Nehemiah, I was given the strategy through prayer, obedience, and seeking His face. After creating the course and prayer journal, people started coming to me for help. I knew that everything they needed was in that course. As people signed up, God prompted me to develop a coaching program. So sometimes God will give the first assignment to see if you are obedient. When He sees that you've done what He asked, He will give the greater assignments. After launching the coaching program, He connected me with someone who gave me the opportunity to speak for the first time, at a youth group about entrepreneurship.

God gave Nehemiah the blueprint to rebuild the walls (Nehemiah 2:18), and in the same way, He gave me the blueprint to build something I had never constructed before.

In that same season, I found myself listening to a pastor teach on the story of Nehemiah. One line stopped me in my tracks: "Anything that lingers in your heart for weeks or months with the same passion is a true purpose." That statement echoed the reality Nehemiah lived. God didn't answer him right away, and perhaps, like the pastor suggested, it was to see whether the passion would fade or remain.

As I reflected, I realized that my burden had actually been with me all year. It didn't just show up suddenly, it had been marinating, quietly pressing on my heart day after day. And I believe that's how purpose often works. It lingers. It grows. It stirs you to tears. It doesn't let you go. And it doesn't always start with clarity; sometimes, it starts with discomfort. So let me ask you: Have you been burdened with a task that God placed on your heart for some time now but you're unsure where or how to start? If so, this chapter is for you.

You may feel unqualified, uncertain, or even overwhelmed. But let Nehemiah's story remind you: the burden is the beginning. The vision will come and the strategy will follow. And the God who gave you the burden will also equip you to carry it to completion. Just as Nehemiah said in Nehemiah 2:18, "I told them how the hand of my God had been favorable to me... and they said, 'Let us arise and build.' So they put their hands to the good work."

It's time to arise and build.

Pray For and Prepare a Strategy

One of the most powerful lessons I've learned on this entrepreneurial journey is this: God is not withholding blessings because He is mean or distant. In fact, it's often the opposite. Sometimes, we're simply not ready. The delay is mercy in disguise. We'll talk more about this in the chapter on *capacity*, but I want to highlight it here because it's foundational to vision-building.

When Nehemiah heard the news of Jerusalem's broken walls, his first response wasn't to act; it was to pray. And not just a "God help me" prayer. He began with *repentance*. Nehemiah 1:6–7 says, *"I confess the sins we Israelites, including myself and my father's family, have committed against you... We have acted very wickedly toward you."* He didn't make excuses. He acknowledged generational sin. He understood that the disobedience of his ancestors had contributed to the destruction around him.

This struck a deep chord with me. As I studied Nehemiah's approach, I felt a conviction to do the same for my own life. I went before God and repented; not only for my own sins, but for the decisions made in my bloodline that may have opened the door to lack, limitation, and poverty. I believe that although salvation through Jesus has made us free, many of us are still walking around with broken-down spiritual and mental walls. We are saved, but exposed. Free, but unfortified.

Walls in Scripture symbolize more than just physical protection; they represent *stability*, *structure*, and *order*. A city without walls was a city in shame. Proverbs 25:28

says, *"A person without self-control is like a city with broken-down walls."* In the New Testament, Paul teaches that some "walls" (or strongholds) need to be torn down. In 2 Corinthians 10:4–5, he writes, *"The weapons of our warfare are not carnal but mighty through God for the pulling down of strongholds..."* This shows us that not all walls (strongholds) are good. Some must be *demolished*, and others must be *rebuilt*. The ones that the enemy builds up around your mind (soul) are the ones that should be torn down. As long as they are up, he can do whatever he wants to your mind. But once we (through the power of the Holy Ghost pull down those walls), we build back new walls by believing and thinking on the good things God says in His word.

So before Nehemiah made a move, he *"cleaned house"* spiritually. Then he prayed for *strategy*. In Nehemiah 1:11, he boldly asked God for favor with the king. He didn't run in the palace empty-handed, nor was he emotionally reactive. Instead, he prepared in prayer. And when the moment came in Nehemiah 2, after about three to four months of waiting, the king noticed his sorrowful face and asked, *"What is it you want?"* (v. 4). But instead of blurting out his needs, Nehemiah paused again—*he prayed silently on the spot.*

Then, in verse 5, he presented a clear, strategic request: *"Send me to the city in Judah where my ancestors are buried so that I can rebuild it."*

If God were to send an investor, a sponsor, a grant writer, or a kingdom connection into your life tomorrow, would you be ready? Would you have a written plan or a clear list of what you need and where you're going? We often pray for provision, but strategy is what ensures we steward provision well.

So here's the challenge: begin to *strategize your plan*. Write the vision down. Make it plain (Habakkuk 2:2). Don't wait until the door opens; prepare now so you'll know exactly what to do when the opportunity arrives.

You Need a Team

Now, some may not agree with this, but if you want to turn a God-given vision into tangible reality, you cannot do it alone. You'll need a team. But not just *any* team, but a *qualified* team. Nehemiah didn't just recruit anybody. He chose people who were *skilled*, *positioned*, and *willing* to carry out the work.

In Nehemiah 2:17–18, he addresses the Jewish leaders, priests, nobles, officials, and skilled workers. But before recruiting them, Nehemiah did something masterful: he *presented the vision with clarity and conviction*. And he followed a 4-part method. These 4 methods can also be used for winning your target clients for sales. But for the purposes of building a team, every visionary, leader and kingdom entrepreneur should pay close attention to:

1. **Identify the Pain Point:** Nehemiah opened with the brutal reality: *"You see the trouble we are in: Jerusalem lies in ruins, and its gates have been burned with fire."* He didn't sugarcoat the issue. He made the need clear, urgent, and collective. He used words like *ruin*, *destroyed*, and *trouble*. Your audience needs to know *why* the work matters.

2. **Empower with Passion:** After laying out the pain, Nehemiah spoke with boldness and fire: *"Come, let us rebuild the wall of Jerusalem, and we will no longer be in disgrace."* (v. 17) He didn't just diagnose the problem, he *inspired* them to become part of the solution. He spoke *with them*, not *at them*.

3. **Call Them to Action:** His call to action was simple and precise: *"Let us rebuild."* He gave them something to *do*, not just something to *feel*. Vision without action leads you nowhere. But vision with direction gives you momentum.

4. **Share Credibility:** Nehemiah didn't rely on his

> title. He shared testimony: *"I also told them about the gracious hand of my God on me and what the king had said to me."* (v. 18) He let them know "this isn't just my idea." God is in this. When people see that God's hand is on your life, they'll be more confident that their effort will not be wasted.

These four elements—pain point, empowerment with passion, a clear call to action, and credibility—are essential for anyone building something significant. Whether you're launching a business, starting a ministry, writing a book, or building a community; this framework helps others *see*, *feel*, and *follow* and *be a part of* the vision.

Now, it's your turn. Pray for strategy. Prepare your plan. Recruit your team. And when God opens the door, walk through it with confidence, knowing you've already done the spiritual and strategic groundwork.

Distractions Come, But Stay Focused

This section is the meat of the matter. If vision gives birth to purpose, and strategy builds the foundation, then focus is what keeps it alive. In Nehemiah chapter 4, we see the intensity of opposition escalate. The work has begun. The people are building. And right on cue: distraction, mockery, and intimidation show up. Sanballat and Tobiah, who initially laughed at Nehemiah to scorn in chapter 2, now become enraged as they witness actual progress (Nehemiah 4:1).

Tobiah even mocks the quality of their work, saying, "If even a fox climbed up on it, he would break down their wall of stones!" (Nehemiah 4:3). But here's what I love: Nehemiah didn't flinch. He didn't clap back. He didn't hold a meeting to defend himself. He prayed.

In Nehemiah 4:4–5, he says,

"Hear us, our God, for we are despised. Turn their insults back on their own heads..."

He did not let the ridicule distract him—he let it drive him deeper into prayer and deeper into the mission.

And then something powerful happens in verse 14. The people had become exhausted. They were carrying burdens, building with one hand and defending themselves with the other (Nehemiah 4:17). Fear and fatigue set in. But Nehemiah, the leader, rises up and declares:

"Don't be afraid of them. Remember the Lord, who is great and awesome, and fight for your families, your sons and your daughters, your wives and your homes." (Nehemiah 4:14 NIV)

This is a word for every builder. To every man and woman of God rising up to build in business, ministry, marriage, or calling. When you become weary and feel like giving up, remember who you're doing it for. Sometimes, God doesn't remove the burden, He gives you a greater reason to carry it.

I appreciate my career as a dental hygienist now when I look in hindsight. I have a better understanding as to why God would allow uncomfortable conditions to arise in work environments. One specific time, I was temping in an office close to home. At the time I was writing my book "Eagle Find Your Voice." With every book I've written so far, God has always given me a unique strategy on how to get it done. With Eagle, Find Your Voice, I would finish my patient's cleaning and have time left before the hour was done. I would ask around and look to see if anything else needed to be done in the office such as cleaning instruments, sweeping, paperwork, etc. If not, He would prompt me to sit and write. In those days, we were still wearing healthcare hats to protect our hair from aerosols. So on days that I was fasting (I was in a serious and lengthy season of consecration at the time), I would go on my breaks, put my airpod in my ears and listen to scriptures, sermons, and worship. God would then give me inspiration from the scripture and a revelation. Then He would say "write". I didn't realize I would be in such a season of testing. There was a woman at that job site who I believe was a practicing witch. She and two other girls would watch me and try to always set me up. They spoke negatively about me to the manager and made me feel like a fool. In all of that, The Lord kept saying "DON'T LOSE YOUR FOCUS." It was hard not to "clap-back" and defend myself at that time, but the fasting helped me to plunge myself into writing even more. Now I can say—to God be all the glory—I have finished writing and publishing that book and it prophetically was the gateway to my writing ministry. Though I was only a temp at that office, I saw how God came to my defense in many ways I can't even count.

In entrepreneurship, especially when you're building something that has kingdom purpose, the enemy will send opposition. And it won't always be obvious. It could come through discouragement, doubt, unexpected health challenges, relational strain, low profits, failed launches, or even spiritual warfare. But you must hold fast to this truth:

"He who began a good work in you will carry it on to completion until the day of Christ Jesus." (Philippians 1:6). This is not the time to quit. When the weight of the work feels too much, take a page from Nehemiah's strategy: Pray through the pressure. (Nehemiah 4:4–5) Set your eyes on legacy. (Nehemiah 4:14) Guard what you're building while you build. (Nehemiah 4:17) Even in the middle of the attack, Nehemiah never stopped building.

And then comes one of the most iconic verses in this entire story—Nehemiah 6:3 (NLT): "I am doing a great work, and I cannot come down."

Sanballat and his crew were relentless. They tried to lure Nehemiah away multiple times, asking for a meeting (really, a setup). But Nehemiah sent back the same response each time: "I can't come down." This verse weighs on me every time. Nehemiah wasn't being arrogant. No, he was focused. He knew that any detour was a distraction. Any meeting not rooted in mission was a waste of time. He knew the assignment was too important, too sacred, and too time-sensitive to entertain nonsense.

That's the level of focus we need in this season.

Napoleon Hill, author of "Think and Grow Rich" quoted *"Set your mind on a definite goal and observe how quickly the world stands aside to let you pass."* Though Hill's writings were heavily built on the philosophy of achievement and self-help, this quote is rooted deeply in the principle of focusing. Become DANGEROUSLY focused on the thing God called you to build. Keep your eyes on that vision, and your ear to the mouth of the Father.

I want you to hear this in your spirit: What you are building is too important for you to stop now. Yes, distractions will come. Yes, the enemy will use people, emotions, even your own doubts to try and slow you down. But don't come down. Don't quit. Don't explain yourself to mockers. Don't let fatigue make you forget the promise.

You may have to pause to pray. You may have to cry. You may need to rest. But do not abandon the wall.

You are doing *a great work*.

Let me lift your hands today, like Aaron and Hur did for Moses, and remind you: You can do this. With God, all things are possible (Matthew 19:26). Not some things. Not most things. All things.

6

SOLOMON'S MILLION DOLLAR SECRET

Have you ever seen those premium business consultants who charge thousands of dollars to ask you just **one** question?

I've seen a few myself. And the truth is, they're often worth every penny. They've built reputations, companies, and client lists that validate their value. So when you get a rare chance to ask someone like that just **one** question, you don't wing it. You think long and hard. You weigh your options. You write it down. You rehearse it. Because that one question could change everything.

Now imagine you had the same opportunity—not with a CEO or consultant—but with **God Himself.** One question. One divine moment. One chance to ask the Almighty anything.

That's exactly what happened to Solomon.

The Divine Offer

Let's revisit that powerful moment in 1 Kings 3.

"That night the Lord appeared to Solomon in a dream, and God said, **'What do you want? Ask, and I will give it to you!'"** **1 Kings 3:5 (NLT)**

What a question. Imagine the God of the universe giving you a blank check. The possibilities are endless. You could ask for money, fame, protection, power, love. Solomon had access to it all. And yet, he asked for something that would multiply everything else: **wisdom**.

"Give me an understanding heart so that I can govern your people well and know the difference between right and wrong. For who by himself is able to govern this great people of yours?" *(1 Kings 3:9, NLT)*

Solomon's request wasn't flashy, but it was strategic. He wasn't thinking small. He was thinking generationally. He recognized the weight of the responsibility before him and knew he couldn't carry it without divine insight. **Wisdom was the secret weapon.**

And God was pleased.

"The Lord was pleased that Solomon had asked for wisdom. So God replied, 'Because you have asked for wisdom in governing my people with justice... I will give you what you asked for! I will give you a wise and understanding heart... And I will also give you what you did not ask for—riches and fame!'"*(1 Kings 3:10–13, NLT)*

The Million Dollar Question

Solomon didn't just ask a question. He asked the **right** question. And in doing so, he unlocked not just wisdom; but wealth, honor, legacy, and divine strategy. That's why I call it **Solomon's Million Dollar Secret.**

What's the takeaway for you? It's this: **You don't need to know everything; just know how to ask the right question to the right Person.**

You may be facing a major decision in business, ministry, or life. You may not know what direction to go, who to hire, when to launch, or how to scale. But you have access to the same God who gave Solomon supernatural wisdom. That same God is ready to answer you.

"If you need wisdom, ask our generous God, and he will give it to you. He will not rebuke you for asking."*(James 1:5, NLT)*

Solomon Saw the Gap

Now let's look at this moment through a business lens. Solomon wasn't just given a spiritual task; he was placed in a practical leadership position. One of the first things Solomon saw was a **gap in the market**—so to speak.

There was a God to be praised—but **no temple** to praise Him in. Worship was taking place in high places, often near altars dedicated to other gods. The system was broken. The infrastructure was lacking. Solomon saw the need and decided to **build what no one else could or would build.**

"Then Solomon began to build the Temple of the Lord in Jerusalem on Mount Moriah... This was the place that the Lord had chosen... to be the site of the Temple."*(2 Chronicles 3:1, NLT)*

His father David had the desire, but not the clearance. Solomon had the commission. That leads me to ask you: **What are you called to build that your parents couldn't?**

- What are you called to establish that your generation has never seen?

- What spiritual or cultural infrastructure are you meant to pioneer?

- What "gap" are you supposed to fill?

This doesn't only apply to business. This applies to your **calling and assignment.** God is raising up modern-day

Solomons who will build platforms, companies, schools, ministries, and movements—not just for profit, but for purpose.

Ask Boldly, Build Fearlessly

Sometimes we delay building because we feel unqualified. We don't know where to start. But the good news is—you don't need to know everything. You need to ask for **wisdom**. Solomon didn't have all the blueprints the night God spoke to him, but the wisdom unlocked every strategy he needed.

And here's another secret: **Most successful people don't know exactly what they're doing.** Many will tell you that their success came from simply taking a risk and adjusting as they moved forward. As believers, we have an advantage; they have instinct; **we have the Holy Spirit.**

Solomon tells us plainly:

"I have observed something else under the sun. The fastest runner doesn't always win the race, and the strongest warrior doesn't always win the battle... It is all decided by chance, by being in the right place at the right time."--**Ecclesiastes 9:11 (NLT)**

In other words, **favor, timing, and boldness** are more powerful than perfection.

So what's stopping you? If God is giving you a divine opportunity, ask Him the million dollar question: **"Lord, give me wisdom."**

God's Wisdom Advances People

You'll notice a pattern in the Bible: when people asked God for direction, He gave them more than just answers; He gave them advancement.

- **Joseph** received divine interpretation for dreams and was promoted to second-in-command in Egypt. *(Genesis 41)*

- **Daniel** was given supernatural insight that made him ten times wiser than the magicians and enchanters of Babylon. *(Daniel 1:20)*

- **Bezalel** was filled with wisdom, ability, and expertise to build the tabernacle of God. *(Exodus 31:2–5)*

These were not just religious experiences—they were **marketplace advancements**.

Wisdom is the currency of elevation in God's system.

Reflection: What Will You Ask?

If God came to you tonight and said, **"What do you want? Ask, and I will give it to you,"** what would you say?

Solomon's million dollar secret wasn't in having the answer. It was asking **for the key.** Wisdom unlocks everything else.

So today, pray boldly. Think strategically. Move courageously.

Ask for wisdom—and then build what only you can build.

7

INVEST TO HARVEST

What you are unwilling to invest will cost you exponentially when you are expecting to harvest.

Ruth's story is a timeless masterclass in sowing and reaping. Her life began in Moab—a land marked by idolatry, sexual immorality, and material prosperity. Ironically, prosperity in Moab existed during a time when Bethlehem, the house of bread, experienced famine. It was against this backdrop that Naomi, her husband Elimelek, and their two sons moved to Moab in search of better economic opportunity. There, Ruth entered the picture. She married into Naomi's family and, for a time, life seemed stable.

But then tragedy struck. Ruth's husband died. So did her brother-in-law. And eventually, Naomi's husband passed as well. Three widows. No hope in sight.

Naomi decided to return to Bethlehem after hearing that the Lord had visited His people again with provision. Ruth, despite Naomi's insistence that she stay in Moab, chose to cling to her. This was the turning point. Ruth's decision to stay wasn't sentimental; it was sacrificial. It was the beginning of an intentional investment.

Investment: Giving What You Don't Have

Ruth left her homeland, her culture, and any possibility of comfort or remarriage to follow an aging woman to a land she had never known. She arrived in Bethlehem as an outsider—poor, widowed, and labeled. "The Moabite woman." "The foreigner." "The one from the pagan country."

She had no money. No inheritance. No status. But she had time. And she gave it.

Ruth chose to invest her labor; gleaning in the fields, humbling herself to pick up the scraps left behind by the harvesters. She wasn't paid, yet she showed up day after day. Her only return was a handful of barley, until Boaz noticed her.

This is where Kairos time meets human diligence. Boaz saw her faithfulness, her character, and her work ethic. He offered her protection, favor, resources, and access. He even instructed his workers to leave extra grain for her on purpose.

When God sees your investment (your time, your energy, your consistency), He releases favor that money can't buy.

Ruth's investment wasn't just about surviving. It was about positioning. It was about aligning her life with God's providential path. She wasn't working the field just for grain—she was unknowingly stepping into generational destiny. She would become the great-grandmother of King David and, eventually, part of the lineage of Christ.

Stock Market Faith: Delayed Gratification, Big Return

When I first heard God speak the phrase "Invest to Harvest," I was in the early stages of learning about financial investments—stocks, ETFs, bonds, even crypto. I noticed a pattern: when the market dropped, fear crept in. Panic selling became common. But those who stayed, those who held their positions and stayed calm through volatility, were often rewarded with exponential returns.

It clicked for me. That's what Ruth did. That's what many entrepreneurs must do. Investing isn't always cute or instantly gratifying. Often, it feels invisible, uncertain, and slow.

But here's the truth: delayed gratification is one of the clearest signs of mature faith. You might not see the results right away, but if you stick with the process—keep showing up, keep sowing seeds—you'll eventually harvest what you planted and then some.

While Orpah (Ruth's sister-in-law) decided to "pull out of the market—leave Naomi and go home—Ruth chose to keep her investments in when the market was low. Grief is a hard thing to endure, but still Ruth chose to stick with Naomi for the long haul. She invested her time and harvested results.

God Is the Ultimate Market Insider

While the world consults analytics, algorithms, and even psychics for direction, kingdom-minded entrepreneurs have an unfair advantage: divine insight.

God still speaks. And yes, He speaks about money, investments, business decisions, timing, and partnerships. I've personally heard testimonies from Christian business leaders who received dreams, visions, or divine nudges about what to invest in, when to pivot, and when to pause.

I even know a pastor who was told by God to pull out of a specific stock—just days before it crashed.

Think about Daniel interpreting dreams in Babylon, or Joseph forecasting famine and leading Egypt through economic recovery. Think about Moses receiving blueprints for building an entire nation. These were kingdom men operating with prophetic intelligence in the marketplace. Why wouldn't God still do that today?

The kingdom of darkness has counterfeit strategies. But we have the Holy Spirit—the true Source of wisdom.

Invest in Yourself, Too

There's another layer to this: investing in you.

This year, your greatest investment might not be in a stock or a business; it may be in your discipline, your education, or your obedience. That might mean saying "No" to things that are good but not God for this season.

Sometimes God will interrupt your routines and comfort zones to call you into consecration and focus. I've had seasons when I couldn't attend social events, travel, or even keep up with familiar yearly traditions because God needed my yes to build what was next. These moments don't always feel spiritual—but they are deeply strategic. For example, A good portion of this book was written in the early hours of the morning before my family woke up and before going to my dental hygiene job.

Time is one of your most valuable currencies. If you don't learn to invest it wisely, you'll pay with regret.

Orpah Turned Back. You Must Not.

Let me remind you—Orpah, Ruth's sister-in-law, chose to return home. She wasn't evil. She just didn't have the capacity to continue. Her story ends there. We never hear about her again.

Ruth pressed on. And because of it, she harvested a husband, wealth, legacy, and purpose.

There will be people in your life who turn back. They'll settle. They'll stop building. They'll quit mid-process. You cannot afford to follow their path. If God has called you to this work, to this mission, to this assignment—you must hold your position.

Someone is waiting for your "*yes*." Let me say this plainly: there are people whose destinies are tied to your obedience. Yes—your *yes* matters.

If I hadn't sat down to write this book, you wouldn't be reading it right now. Maybe someone else could have written something similar; but your breakthrough might be buried in this chapter, this moment.

So don't back down. Don't procrastinate. Don't delay.

Final Word: What Will You Harvest?

Ruth harvested grain. Then she harvested wealth. Then she harvested love. All from a decision to invest time when she had nothing else to give.

So I ask you:

What can you invest today? What do you need to walk away from so you can go all in? What field are you called to glean in; even if it's barley season? What could you harvest if you committed to the process?

Because in God's economy, seed time and harvest never fail.

And your harvest is coming.

8

GLEANING AND MENTORSHIP

"Let me go out into the harvest fields to pick up the stalks of grain left behind by anyone who is kind enough to let me do it."
— **Ruth 2:2, NLT**

There is a divine strategy in gleaning and placing yourself where wisdom, wealth, and opportunity have already flowed. There is also a divine strategy in asking God to allow the leftovers to fall into your lap until you are the one leaving overflow for others.

This is what Ruth did.

She told Naomi, "Let me go into the fields and glean what's left behind." She wasn't demanding to be the boss. She wasn't trying to harvest the fields on day one. She wasn't pretending to be further along than she was. Ruth embraced her current position with a posture of humility and hunger.

In ancient times, gleaning was reserved for the poor. It wasn't glamorous. It was the work of the overlooked, the outcast, the needy. But Ruth didn't let the stigma of gleaning stop her. She said, "Let me glean." In fact, because she was willing to go where the harvesters already had been, she eventually caught the eye of Boaz, the landowner himself.

Ruth was smart: she got around those who were already reaping. She placed herself in a position to watch, to learn, and to receive. That's the heart posture you need when God is growing you; especially in business.

Gleaning Is a Business Strategy

There was a season in my life when I worked as a temporary dental hygienist. I wasn't tied to one office. I filled in wherever needed; sometimes for a day, sometimes for a year. I was a modern-day gleaner. No practice was "mine," but God used that flexibility to expose me to environments I never would have seen otherwise.

One of the most impactful assignments I had was in a prestigious, wealthy town in my state. You could feel the money in the air. The streets were lined with stores where nothing costs under $700; and that's *if* you were lucky. For some, that might feel intimidating. But I was fascinated. I'll never forget hopping off the train and turning the corner on that luxury street. I had the biggest smile on my face, jokingly singing to myself:

"I think I'm gonna like it here,"

like I was Annie entering a whole new world.

Was I shopping in those stores? No.

Did I feel out of place? Not at all.

I was on assignment. I was gleaning.

Most of my patients were either upper-middle class or flat-out wealthy. Some were quiet about it. You'd never know unless they told you. Others wore their money like a perfume, and let's just say, it didn't always smell good. But no matter how they carried their wealth, I saw every interaction as a divine opportunity.

I made a habit of asking every investor, entrepreneur, or high-level executive one simple question:

"What's the best advice you'd give to a new entrepreneur, investor, or someone looking to climb the ladder in their corporate job?"

And 9 times out of 10, they were happy to share. It gave them a sense of pride, but it gave me a transfer of wisdom. I couldn't afford to be that close to legacy, influence, and impact and not ask for the secret sauce.

This was my Ruth moment. I was gleaning behind the harvesters. They had already built businesses, made mistakes, learned lessons--and here I was, a willing learner.

The Wisdom of Mentorship

Some months later in late November, I began to ask God a deeper question:

"Who should I be listening to right now?"

I didn't want to get swept up in the lights and music of the holiday season and miss my next level of growth. I needed direction for the new year.

And one morning, as I was waking up, I had a quick vision of two women's faces overlapping. I knew them both. I had listened to them before, but never deeply followed their strategies. I immediately knew that they were who I was supposed to glean from in that season. In the next chapter, we will talk more about mentorship and coaching. I believe gleaning is less direct than mentorship. It puts you in proximity but not for a long and extended period of time to truly learn.

You can glean from a distance, and then eventually go a step further to mentorship. You can do this by buying their books, listening to podcasts, doing their training, or listening to their teachings. Don't despise those moments. Don't underestimate the power of exposure.

When You Don't Feel Qualified

Maybe you're in a position right now where you're watching others win. They're building businesses, getting brand deals, traveling, hiring teams. And you're just trying to figure out how to set up an email list. Listen—**glean**!

Ask questions.

Watch patterns.

Get close.

Stay humble.

Take notes.

Even if you can't buy the whole course, buy the e-book. If you can't afford the mentorship program, binge their free YouTube channel. And when God *does* give you the opportunity to connect with someone ahead of you, don't shy away.

"Boaz went over and said to Ruth, 'Listen, my daughter. Stay right here with us when you gather grain; don't go to any other fields.'"

— Ruth 2:8, NLT

Boaz noticed Ruth because she was in the right field. And because she was willing to glean, she gained favor and divine protection. She was elevated not by striving but by alignment.

The system of gleaning was created to feed the poor, but Ruth used it to access her future. What was meant for survival became her strategy for increase.

Don't Despise Your Entry Point

Sometimes, the job you despise…

The family connection you've written off…

An opportunity that doesn't seem prestigious…

…may be the very gateway to your breakthrough.

Gleaning is not glamorous, but it is God-ordained. The harvest doesn't start with ownership; it starts with obedience. You don't need to be the richest, the smartest, or the most qualified. You just need to be present and positioned.

So ask God,

"Whose field should I be gleaning in right now?"

And when He answers you, show up, stay sharp, and get every drop of wisdom you can.

Because gleaners today are harvesters tomorrow.

9

LITTLE BY LITTLE

I remember coming home from high school one day to the sound of a television ad playing in the living room. I can't recall who the ad was from, but I'll never forget the question they asked:

"If you could choose between getting one million dollars today or a penny that doubles every day for 30 days, which would you choose?"

Without hesitation, I said, "The million dollars!" I mean, who wouldn't?

But now, with more wisdom and life experience, I realize the better answer is the penny doubled every day. Why? Because of the "snowball effect; **Law of Accumulation**. Karl Marx profoundly spoke about theory and Henyrk Grossman later continued to expound on it.

Let's look at **Ecclesiastes 11:3 (KJV):**

"If the clouds be full of rain, they empty themselves upon the earth."

Notice what it doesn't say: "At the first drop, the cloud empties." No, the Scripture teaches us about process. Time. Waiting. The cloud fills **first**, and **then** it pours.

In scientific terms, rain occurs when water droplets accumulate inside a cloud until it becomes too heavy. Gravity pulls the water down, and we get rainfall. But before that, there's accumulation. Quiet, steady, invisible accumulation.

The Curse of Instant Gratification

A couple of months ago, I caught myself saying something that sounded funny and trendy:

"I like instant gratification."

It rolled off my tongue so easily. But before I knew it, it started showing up in my life like an uninvited guest. I'd spend double on items I could've saved on had I waited. I'd choose convenience over wisdom. Eventually, I had to **repent**. I know that may sound intense, but hear me out.

How many doors could God have opened if we chose **delayed gratification** instead of impulsive decisions?

Instant gratification is subtle. It sneaks into our eating habits, our spending, our discipline. Think about it:

- Eating a whole pack of cookies when you're trying to lose weight.

- Napping instead of submitting that assignment.

- Scrolling on social media for hours instead of creating the content that could've grown your brand.

Each of these moments feels small, but they accumulate too, just in the wrong direction.

Applying the Law to Wealth & Entrepreneurship

This principle is just as relevant in your business as it is in your personal growth. Let's look at investing. When you get paid, the temptation is to spend immediately. But if you take a portion and invest it—whether in stocks, savings, or business development—you activate **compound growth**.

The first deposit may feel like nothing happened. In fact, if you need instant results, you'll likely pull that money back out. But if you can **wait**, if you can **endure the process**, the Law of Accumulation will begin to work for you.

This is the same with building your brand or growing your business. When you first begin posting on social media, creating content, and writing emails, it feels like you're speaking into the void. But keep going. Every post is a drop in the cloud. One day, that cloud will burst, and your breakthrough will rain down.

Think of **Nehemiah** and the wall. He didn't build it overnight. It happened **brick by brick**. Each moment of labor looked small and maybe even insignificant. But the, one day, they stood back and the wall was done.

That's the Law of Accumulation.

Solomon Knew This Too

In the same chapter of Ecclesiastes, Solomon says:

"Send your grain across the seas, and in time, profits will flow back to you. But divide your investments among many places, for you do not know what risks might lie ahead."(**Ecclesiastes 11:1–2, NLT**)

Don't eat your grain. **Send it**. Invest it. Watch for return over **time**. He even uses **water** imagery (grain across seas) because money should always be in **flow**. It's why we call it "currency." It should move, not sit stagnant.

And it gets even better: Solomon advises to **diversify**. Multiple "streams" of income are wise because life brings uncertainty. If one stream slows, another can keep you afloat.

Final Thoughts

Don't despise the day of small beginnings. Don't curse the delay, **bless it**. Because in the delay, God is **filling your clouds**. In the waiting, He is preparing your overflow.

Choose the penny over the million. Choose process over impulse. Choose to build brick by brick, and soon you'll look up and realize, you've built something worth raining down.

Delay is not denial. It's just accumulation.

Let your cloud get full.

10

WHAT'S IN YOUR HAND?

Exodus 4 teaches us a profound and often overlooked truth: your God-given intelligence, skills, and gifts speak louder than your words. They were not given to you randomly—they were given intentionally, with purpose, power, and destiny in mind.

We've already discussed this in the chapter on Leverage: what we often perceive as a limitation may actually be the very tool God wants to use to elevate us to the next level. But in this chapter, let's go deeper into another key principle:

The power of starting small.

We love to dream about the big blessings, the distant future, the "one day" visions. But what about the little and near blessings? The things we already have, already carry, and often overlook? That's where God wants to begin.

Let's zoom in on Moses' story. In Exodus 4, Moses is standing before God at the burning bush, expressing why he's not qualified to lead Israel. He's anxious, insecure, and convinced that his flaws make him unfit for the mission.

"But Moses protested again, 'What if they won't believe me or listen to me? What if they say, "The Lord never appeared to you"?'" *(Exodus 4:1, NLT)*

God responds with a question that seems almost off-topic:

"Then the Lord asked him, 'What is that in your hand?' 'A shepherd's staff,' Moses replied." *(Exodus 4:2, NLT)*

At first glance, it might feel like God is brushing Moses off. It's as if He's ignoring the real issue. But He's not. God is redirecting Moses' attention from what he lacks to what he already has.

That ordinary rod; just a shepherd's staff became one of the most powerful instruments in Israel's history. In God's hands, that rod would:

- Turn into a serpent before Pharaoh

- Strike the Nile and turn its water to blood

- Part the Red Sea

- Bring water from a rock

- Win battles as it was raised in Moses' hands

It wasn't about the rod; it was about what God could do through what Moses already had.

Many of us are holding something right now that seems ordinary or insignificant. A skill, a talent, a tool, or even just a deep passion. But what if that "thing" is a seed? God often gives gifts in seed form. They seem small, raw, undeveloped, but packed full of potential.

"Do not despise these small beginnings, for the Lord rejoices to see the work begin…" *(Zechariah 4:10, NLT)*

A seed looks unimpressive, but planted, watered, and nurtured, it becomes a tree that bears fruit. Then that fruit comes with more seeds. One seed multiplied over time can become an entire forest. But here's the key: seeds don't grow when they stay in your hand. They only grow when they are planted in faith.

What's in your hand may not look like much, but in God's economy, that gift—when surrendered—can unlock breakthroughs for you and others. But you must steward it. Take inventory. Offer it to God.

Stop Focusing on What You Lack.

Let's be honest, Moses' excuses sound a lot like ours.

"But Moses pleaded with the Lord, 'O Lord, I'm not very good with words... I get tongue-tied, and my words get tangled.'" *(Exodus 4:10, NLT)*

Sound familiar?

- *I'm not ready.*

- *I don't have the platform.*

- *No one will listen to me.*

- *What if I fail?*

But worse than what other people think about you is what you think about yourself. Insecurity can be louder than the enemy's voice, and far more dangerous if left unchecked. But God doesn't need your perfection. He needs your obedience.

"But the Lord said to him, 'Who makes a person's mouth? Who decides whether people speak or do not speak...? Is it not I, the Lord? Now go! I will be with you as you speak, and I will instruct you in what to say.'" -- **Exodus 4:11–12 (NLT)**

God already factored your weaknesses into His calling on your life. The question is: will you trust Him enough to start with what you have?

What's in Your House?

Let's pivot to another story that drives this point home. In 2 Kings 4, a widow approaches the prophet Elisha in desperation. Her husband has died, and creditors are coming to take her sons as payment. She's overwhelmed, grieving, and broke.

Elisha's response?

"'Tell me, what do you have in the house?' 'Nothing at all, except a flask of olive oil,' she replied." -- **2 Kings 4:2 (NLT)**

She almost missed it: "nothing at all…except." That little exception was her breakthrough in disguise. Elisha gives her a strategy: gather empty jars, shut the door, and start pouring. And the oil did not run out until she ran out of vessels.

"When she told the man of God what had happened, he said to her, 'Now sell the olive oil and pay your debts, and you and your sons can live on what is left over.'" -- **2 Kings 4:7 (NLT)**

Her miracle wasn't in something new; it was in something she already had, but overlooked. Her house held the seed for her financial breakthrough.

Let me ask you now: What's in your house? What's that thing you've been dismissing as too small, too common, or not enough?

Maybe it's:

- A love for writing

- A skill in baking or teaching

- A burden for youth

- A passion for organization

- A mind for business or marketing

- A creative flair for content or design

Don't bury it. Don't belittle it. Bring it to God. Let Him breathe on it. And with His guidance, bring that thing to the marketplace and multiply it.

"God has given each of you a gift from his great variety of spiritual gifts. Use them well to serve one another." -- **1 Peter 4:10 (NLT)**

Surrender is the Key

What's the turning point in both of these stories?

Surrender.

Moses didn't become perfect, but he became willing. The widow didn't have riches, but she used what she had in obedience. That's all God asks. He doesn't need your perfection, He needs your *surrender*.

"Now all glory to God, who is able, through his mighty power at work within us, to accomplish infinitely more than we might ask or think." *(Ephesians 3:20, NLT)*

When you surrender what's in your hand (your rod, your oil, your gift) you make room for God's supernatural multiplication.

Reflection & Activation: Take Inventory

Before you move on, pause and ask yourself:
- What's in my hand?
- What's in my house?
- What skill, gift, or idea have I been ignoring?
- What seed am I holding that needs to be planted?

Write them down. Pray over them. Ask the Lord how to activate and steward them. Then start small, start now, and trust God for the rest.

11

THE PARABLE OF THE TALENTS

If I could choose a single scripture that speaks directly to business, entrepreneurship, and scaling with divine purpose, I'd inevitably choose the Parable of the Talents (Matthew 25:14–30). It's a story Jesus told His disciples that should forever change the way Kingdom-minded believers view and do business.

Jesus described a nobleman—symbolic of Himself—who was about to leave for a long journey. But before going, He entrusted His wealth to three of His servants. "He gave five bags of silver to one, two bags of silver to another, and one bag of silver to the last—dividing it in proportion to their abilities. He then left on his trip" (Matthew 25:15, NLT). Each servant received something. No one was left empty-handed. That alone is a revelation: God never sends us into life or business empty. Everyone has something to start with.

The first two servants immediately went to work. "The servant who received the five bags of silver began to invest the money and earned five more. The servant with two bags of silver also went to work and earned two more" (Matthew 25:16–17, NLT). But the third servant took a different approach. Out of fear, he buried his one bag of silver in the ground. He played it safe. When the master returned, he rewarded the ones who had multiplied what was entrusted to them, but he harshly rebuked the one who did nothing.

What's powerful about this parable is not only the financial stewardship it teaches, but the command Jesus gives. Luke 19:13 gives a parallel to this parable: *"Before he left, he called together ten of his servants and divided among them ten pounds of silver, saying, 'Invest this for me while I am gone'"* **(Luke 19:13, NLT).** The King James Version famously puts it this way: **"Occupy until I come."**

At first glance, the word *occupy* might seem like a passive term; just holding down the fort, staying busy, or being content with what you have. But when you dig into the original language, the command comes alive with purpose.

The Hidden Power in "Occupy"

The Hebrew and Aramaic root word for "occupy" is **yarash**, which means *to possess, to inherit, to take, or to dispossess.* This is not passive language—it's the language of conquest. The same word is used when God told the Israelites to possess the Promised Land. In other words, to *occupy* meant to *take territory.*

The Greek word used in Luke is πραγματεύομαι (**pragmateuomai**) which means *to do business, to trade, to negotiate, to engage in commerce.* From this Greek word we get the English word "pragmatic," which hints at practical, results-oriented action. This is not just a call to be spiritual; it's a call to be strategic.

So when Jesus says, "Occupy until I come," He is literally saying, **"Do business until I return. Take territory. Multiply what I gave you. Be active. Engage the culture. Dominate in the marketplace."**

The man with five talents obeyed this command by engaging in transactions that yielded five more. He moved his money. He understood something that we must embrace as Kingdom entrepreneurs: **money is called "currency" because it is meant to flow.** As we explored in the chapter "Little by Little," wealth is not just about accumulation, it's about *circulation.*

The servant who buried his talent misunderstood the Master. He thought caution was wisdom. He equated playing it safe with being responsible. But God's Kingdom rewards movement, not maintenance.

--Matthew 25:26–27 (NLT).

Doing Business in the Spirit and the Natural

This story is a wake-up call for CEOs, entrepreneurs, leaders, and visionaries. You have been given something: an idea, a strategy, a skill set, a team, a brand, a platform. The question is: What are you doing with it?

You can't afford to sit on your resources, afraid of loss or criticism. Don't let the fear of failure bury your calling. Don't keep your talent or capital in a savings account collecting dust when God has called you to invest and multiply.

Let's be practical:

- You can't be afraid to invest in the business God gave you.

- You can't be afraid to hire quality workers who will 10x your results.

- You can't be afraid to pursue partnerships with people God has divinely connected you to.

- You can't be afraid to launch the course, build the

product, or enter the market.

Why? Because unlike the world, we have a divine advantage. **We have the Ultimate Nobleman—Jesus Christ—who is all-knowing, all-seeing, and all-powerful.** He knows the market. He knows the economic trends. He knows the timing. And He is willing to reveal divine strategies if we ask.

"If you need wisdom, ask our generous God, and he will give it to you. He will not rebuke you for asking." **--James 1:5 (NLT).**

Our businesses should be prophetic and powerful. As Spirit-filled believers, we're not just making money, we're building Kingdom infrastructure. God can lead you into the right investment, the right timing, the right market, and the right audience. That's the kind of insight no MBA or market analyst can provide.

Business as a Tool for Souls

But let's not stop at wealth and wisdom. Here's the greater reality: **our businesses are also tools for evangelism.** Through our products, services, and communication, we're not just winning clients—we're winning souls.

The marketplace is not just a place to build wealth; it's a place to build the Kingdom.

"Yes, each of you should use whatever gift you have received to serve others, as faithful stewards of God's grace in its various forms" (1 Peter 4:10, NLT).

So, what's the real return on investment? It's not just five more talents. It's five more souls. Five more families were restored. Five more women were empowered. Five more communities transformed. Business is a gateway to ministry when done God's way.

Occupy Until He Comes

Friend, Jesus is returning—and He's looking for a return on what He gave you. He's not coming for idle believers. He's coming for faithful stewards. He's coming for Kingdom entrepreneurs who turned ideas into influence and influence into impact.

So, take the talent. Trade it. Multiply it. Build with it. Risk with it. Invest with it. Let your obedience be your offering.

"To those who use well what they are given, even more will be given, and they will have an abundance" --**Matthew 25:29 (NLT).**

Occupy. Do business. Take territory. Until He comes.

SCALE YOUR BUSINESS

12

God's Divine Strategy

God's presence is the starting point for everything. It's the starting point for your purpose, your strategy, and your success. When you align your heart and will with His, He not only gives you vision, He gives you the **resources** you'll need. He will also give you the **timing**, and **people** you need to bring that vision to life. Divine strategy is not just about having good ideas; it's about receiving **God-ideas** that put you in alignment with His will and ahead of worldly systems.

Whenever someone asks me, "How do I know what I'm supposed to be doing?" I always say, "Get in the presence of God." That answer might sound cliché, but the presence of God is not basic. You'll never leave there the same way you entered. Exchanges happen in His presence if you are willing to stay long enough to hear Him.

When you spend time with God, you receive direction. Even when others are panicking, you're preparing. When others are downsizing, you're scaling with confidence. His divine strategy becomes your advantage.

God's Timing Is a Strategy

In *Exodus 12*, we find one of the most profound examples of God's divine strategy. Egypt was about to experience the final plague: the death of the firstborn. But God had a **detailed escape plan** for Israel. Not only would they leave Egypt, but they would do so safely, with their families intact, and with the wealth of their enemies in hand.

"From now on, this month will be the first month of the year for you." — *Exodus 12:2, NLT*

God **restructured their calendar**. He shifted their time to match His timeline. This shows us something powerful: when God is releasing a strategy, He may also **reset your windows of time**. While others may be slowing down, He might tell you to speed up—or vice versa. The key is to **be sensitive to His timing**.

When I was pregnant with my son, God spoke to me months in advance. He told me that I was also "pregnant" with another baby: a book. I knew it was time-sensitive. As soon as I gave birth to my son, it was then time to "push out the book" shortly after. I had my son in January and by mid February I was writing my book. God gave me a unique strategy on how to juggle my new season as a mom of two and writing this book. He prompted me into a consecration every weekend until the end of March. He gave me an unprecedented kind of strength to stay up through the night writing, and to press through like I was birthing in the spirit. To the glory of God, the book was completed within that time window. It was not about convenience. It was about obedience to **divine timing**.

Strategic Instructions Lead to Supernatural Protection

God didn't just give Israel a vague direction. He gave them **specific instructions**, including how to prepare a meal and mark their homes.

"They are to take some of the blood and smear it on the sides and top of the doorframes of the houses where they eat the animal."

— Exodus 12:7, NLT

"But the blood on your doorposts will serve as a sign, marking the houses where you are staying. When I see the blood, I will pass over you."

— Exodus 12:13, NLT

Think of this as a divine **business survival strategy**. While the economy (Egypt) was experiencing judgment and death, Israel was covered. In modern language: your business may be "marked with the blood." While others are folding in a tough market, God is keeping you afloat, growing, and even **thriving**. This is all because you followed His strategy. His covering is on your house.

Meal Plans and Market Plans

God also gave Israel a **meal plan**: how to roast the lamb, how to eat it with bitter herbs, and what to wear. These were not random details. This was preparation for movement.

"These are your instructions for eating this meal: Be fully dressed, wear your sandals, and carry your walking stick in your hand. Eat the meal with urgency, for this is the Lord's Passover."

— *Exodus 12:11, NLT*

Let this speak prophetically into your business: **What is your God-given meal plan?** What has He told you to feed on or pull away from? What has He told you to study, invest in, release, or sell?

I went to a business conference one year and the speaker compared *social media* to *sugar*. "How interesting," I thought. It's sweet and makes you feel good in the moment, but it can be addicting, and can cause a sudden "sugar crash." How many times do we feel depleted of energy after scrolling endlessly on social media? The time and energy stolen from being distracted could have been used to promote your business. So essentially, we need to cut out excessive sugar." When was the last time we refreshed ourselves by quenching our thirst with *the water of the Word*?

There have been many times where God put me on a physical meal plan in order to carry out time sensitive and high focus projects. A few months ago, I was working on a client's book that required meticulous attention to detail. He told me to cut out heavy starches and eat protein, fruits and vegetable based foods. Things that naturally boosted my energy and gave me the mental bandwidth needed to focus.

Jacob's Divine Strategy: Multiplying What Shouldn't Multiply

Another striking example of divine strategy is Jacob and Laban's story. After years of serving his father-in-law Laban, Jacob was ready to establish his own household. The deal seemed unfair; he would only take the spotted and blemished animals, while Laban kept the strong, pure-colored ones.

But then God stepped in.

"During the mating season, I once had a dream in which I saw that the male goats mating with the females were streaked, speckled, and spotted."

— Genesis 31:10, NLT

"In that dream, the angel of God said to me... 'Look up, and you will see that only the streaked, speckled, and spotted males are mating with the females of your flock.'"

— Genesis 31:11–12, NLT

God gave Jacob a **vision**, literally. A divine insight that defied the natural order of breeding. That insight made him **wealthy** in a short period of time. What looked like a disadvantage was turned into a **set-up for supernatural increase**.

Let that encourage you: God still gives business strategy through dreams, visions, and specific instructions. What the world counts out, God counts in. He will give you an edge if you stay aligned with Him.

Divine Strategy Always Includes Obedience

Both Moses and Jacob had to do something that seemed strange. Moses had to **paint doorposts with blood**. Jacob had to **strip branches and place them in water troughs**. Neither made sense in the natural. But strategy from heaven rarely does.

God may give you an instruction that doesn't fit your five-year plan. He may ask you to launch something in a season that looks like a drought. He may call you to invest in something when others are pulling back. Trust Him. Just like how He instructed me to push out a book and instructed my husband and I to prepare an event while we had a newborn. Don't be surprised if He comes knocking on the door of your heart with unprecedented instructions.

"Trust in the Lord with all your heart; do not depend on your own understanding. Seek his will in all you do, and he will show you which path to take."

— Proverbs 3:5–6, NLT

Your understanding is not your compass, His presence is.

Final Thoughts: Follow the Cloud, Not the Crowd

As the children of Israel left Egypt, they didn't walk blindly. God gave them strategy not just for escape, but for their **journey forward**.

"The Lord went ahead of them. He guided them during the day with a pillar of cloud, and he provided light at night with a pillar of fire. This allowed them to travel by day or by night."

— Exodus 13:21, NLT

He didn't just get them out, He led them forward.

Let God do the same for you. Don't chase what everyone else is doing. Follow His presence. In His presence is not only peace; it's precision. It's the cloud that leads, the fire that illuminates, and the strategy that sustains.

Action Step:

- Ask God to reveal His divine strategy for your next season.

- Fast, pray, and sit quietly in His presence.

- Journal the instructions you receive, no matter how small they may seem.

- Take action with boldness. The presence of God is your compass and your advantage.

Remember: Divine strategy will always outlast man-made systems. When you follow God's blueprint, He will lead you into abundance, protection, and purpose every time.

13

EATING THE CRUMBS

For any entrepreneur starting out, or even one who's been at it for a while but hasn't quite broken into profitability—here's a counterintuitive but powerful principle for growth: eat the crumbs.

We tend to think of crumbs as insignificant, the leftovers that fall from the real feast. But in the right hands, crumbs can be the catalyst for breakthrough. They may be small, but they are still pieces of the whole. And sometimes, a crumb is all you need to change your life.

The Canaanite Woman and the Crumbs

Let's visit the powerful story in **Matthew 15:25–28**:

"Then came she and worshipped him, saying, Lord, help me. But he answered and said, It is not meet to take the children's bread, and to cast it to dogs. And she said, Truth, Lord: yet the dogs eat of the crumbs which fall from their masters' table. Then Jesus answered and said unto her, O

woman, great is thy faith: be it unto thee even as thou wilt. And her daughter was made whole from that very hour."

This woman was not part of the intended group Jesus was ministering to at the time; she was a Gentile, a Canaanite. By all accounts, she was disqualified. She wasn't "in the room," wasn't on the list, wasn't among the chosen.

Yet, **she dared to believe that even the crumbs held power.**

She didn't demand the whole loaf. She wasn't offended when Jesus used strong language to describe the priorities of His mission. She acknowledged the truth, but she also leaned on the deeper truth: *that a crumb from the Master's table still came from the Master.*

Crumbs in the Business World: Free Masterclasses and Webinars

For entrepreneurs, the *crumbs* are everywhere: **free masterclasses, webinars, YouTube videos, blog posts, podcasts, and challenges**. They are the entry-level content offered by experienced coaches, consultants, and creators. Many times, these free offerings are created to whet your appetite; to entice you to buy the full course or coaching package. But don't despise these crumbs. **Eat**

them. Learn from them. Let them feed your mind and stir your hunger.

When I started my business journey, this is exactly what I did. I couldn't afford the full bread. Those premium coaching programs, VIP days, the masterminds, and high-end digital courses were completely out of my budget. I was only a few years out of college. Tenoy and I were starting a new chapter in our lives as homeowners and pregnant with our first baby. I was just building steady income from my dental hygiene career. I couldn't splurge the way I wanted to. But I *could* show up for the free Zoom trainings. I *could* register for every free business bootcamp I could find. I *could* follow thought leaders and take notes on their free value-packed content.

Was it everything? No. Was it enough to begin? Absolutely.

The crumbs gave me a taste. They woke up my entrepreneurial palate. They showed me what was possible. They also gave me clarity on what I liked, what I didn't, what resonated, and what didn't fit my God-given calling. Over time, I began to see patterns. I began to discern quality. And I began to build.

Crumbs Are Not a Lifetime Diet

Now let's be clear: crumbs are for *starting*, not for *staying*.

Too many entrepreneurs try to build million-dollar businesses on free advice. That's not wise stewardship. It's like a bride showing up at her wedding with 50 flavors of cake samples instead of picking one to serve her guests. **Crumbs are for tasting, not for feasting.**

Eventually, you will have to invest. You will need to sit at the table. You will need to buy the bread.

But starting with crumbs allows you to test before you commit. It gives you insight without the overwhelm of large financial investments. It also allows you to start moving, and movement is the key to momentum.

AB Testing Your Growth Strategy

Once you've digested enough crumbs to have a sense of what niche, message, or product you're leaning toward. So now, you start AB testing.

Try different types of content. Experiment with social media formats. Test two headlines for the same offer. See what kind of posts resonate with your audience. Let the crumbs **lead you to data** and let the data **lead you to strategy.**

Faith, Hunger, and Business Breakthrough

Like the Canaanite woman, there's a kind of holy hunger that gets God's attention. She was bold, but not arrogant. Hungry, but humble. She didn't let being "outside the room" stop her from receiving what she needed.

That kind of hunger is honored in heaven, and it works in business too. God rewards diligence. He rewards those who will search, seek, knock, and ask; even when they have no budget, no followers, and no formal business background.

So, if you're in a "crumbs" season, don't despise it. **Use it. Eat the crumbs. Let them nourish your faith.**

Eventually, you'll move from eating at the edge of the table...to sitting at the table. To owning the table. To inviting others to the table.

But for now, be faithful with the crumbs. That's where all great stories begin.

14

THE POWER OF LEVERAGE

In both business and personal life, **leverage** is the bridge between old limitations and new levels. It stems from the God-given principle of multiplication. The practice of using a little to access a lot. When rightly applied, leverage allows you to stop working harder and start working *wiser*, with less strain and more supernatural gain.

Leverage in Scarcity: Elijah and the Widow at Zarephath

"Then the word of the Lord came to him, saying, 'Arise, go to Zarephath, which belongs to Sidon, and dwell there. See, I have commanded a widow there to provide for you.'"
—1 Kings 17:8–9 (NKJV)

Elijah had just come from the brook Cherith, where he was fed by ravens during a drought. But when the brook dried up, God instructed him to go to a widow in Zarephath; a woman who was down to her last meal.

This widow had nothing but a handful of flour and a little oil in a jar. She was preparing to cook a final meal for herself and her son before dying. But Elijah gave her a divine key:

"Do not fear... make me a small cake from it first, and bring it to me; and afterward make some for yourself and your son."

—1 Kings 17:13 (NKJV)

What seemed like a harsh demand was actually an invitation to access *leverage*. The little she had, when yielded to God through the prophet, became the source of ongoing provision:

"The bin of flour was not used up, nor did the jar of oil run dry, according to the word of the Lord which He spoke by Elijah."

—1 Kings 17:16 (NKJV)

Entrepreneurship and the Need for Leverage

Entrepreneurship comes with its set of challenges. It's something you'll need tenacity and resilience for. However, no matter how hard it gets, there are always ways to use leverage to get better. Leverage is highly important because it helps you reach places with less time, energy, and skill than what would have been needed if done alone.

I remember watching a show one day and the opening 10-second rustic scene led me to have a *eureka* moment. An English midwife was riding her bike to a patient's home. While people were walking down the same street as she was, she reached her destination nearly three times faster—not because she was faster or stronger, but because she had *leverage*. The bicycle multiplied the speed of her movement.

It doesn't mean she was more powerful or more gifted than those walking. It simply means she had something working to her advantage. The same idea applies when flying versus driving. Driving from New York to Florida can take 15+ hours, but flying from New York to Florida? Under two hours. That's the power of leveraged transportation, and the principle works the same in business.

As an entrepreneur, you must first know your industry. Then, you must discern what kind of leverage will serve you best. Is it social media? Paid ads? YouTube? ChatGPT? Networking events? A software system that automates tasks you'd otherwise do manually? Or maybe a mix of them. When you identify and implement the right leverage, you can start or scale your business faster and more effectively.

What systems of automation and optimization can you implement today? What gifts or "quirks" do you have that might actually be hidden advantages?

It's said that **Michael Phelps**, the most decorated Olympian in history, wasn't just skilled, he was literally *built* for swimming. While he stands at 6 feet 4 inches, his torso is proportioned like that of a 6'8" man, and his legs are shorter than average. This unique combination gives him extraordinary swimming leverage in the water. What others might view as physical imbalance was actually his *advantage*.

In the same way, many people overlook their natural leverage—whether it's charisma, discipline, creativity, or empathy. Your advantage might be the very trait you've been trying to downplay. Some people are extremely relational and warm. That's leverage for coaching or ministry. Others are analytical and focused. That's leverage for strategy, teaching, or finance.

Leverage is a Kingdom Principle

- **David** used a slingshot and a stone to defeat Goliath (1 Samuel 17).

- **Moses** lifted a rod to part the Red Sea (Exodus 14:16).

- **Jesus** used five loaves and two fish to feed thousands (Matthew 14:13–21).

Each example shows us that God isn't limited by quantity. He is the ultimate lever! In Business, whether your leverage is digital tools, divine favor, or disciplined habits, God will use it to maximize your impact.

Leverage, Catalyst, and the Favor Factor

As we've journeyed through this chapter, we've focused deeply on the word "leverage." It's a powerful tool in both business and life. It's a way to do more with less, to gain traction and momentum faster than what could be accomplished alone. But if I could introduce one more word that complements and amplifies leverage for the believer, it would be this: "catalyst."

Both leverage and catalyst share a similar end goal—to make progress faster, easier, and more efficient. And in a world where time is one of the most precious commodities we have, understanding both is vital. What is wasted cannot be recovered. So how do we, as Kingdom entrepreneurs and leaders, operate in ways that honor time and steward it well?

We partner with leverage (systems, people, tools, and strategies) and we trust God to be our catalyst.

If I were to draw a parallel between scripture and these two concepts, I would align "favor with man" to leverage, and "favor with God" to catalyst.

"And Jesus grew in wisdom and stature, and in favor with God and man." —Luke 2:52 (NIV)

Favor with man—relationships, mentors, collaborations, platforms—these are the leverage points that God can use to elevate us. But favor with God is the catalyst. It's the supernatural acceleration that causes time to collapse. It's divine momentum that brings you into places and promotions you never saw coming.

A catalyst, by definition, speeds up a reaction without being changed by it. And isn't that just like our God? He steps into a situation, shifts everything in your favor, *yet He Himself remains constant.* God never changes, yet everything changes when He steps in.

Elijah Outruns a Chariot: Supernatural catalysts

In 1 Kings 18, we find a stunning example of leverages and catalysts. After years of famine, God told Elijah that rain was coming. He then sent word to King Ahab:

"Go up, eat and drink; for there is the sound of abundance of rain."

—1 Kings 18:41 (NKJV)

Elijah warned Ahab to get in his chariot and hurry to Jezreel before the rain caught him. Naturally, Ahab should've arrived first. He had horses and wheels (CHARIOTS). But then something extraordinary happened:

"Then the hand of the Lord came upon Elijah; and he girded up his loins and ran ahead of Ahab to the entrance of Jezreel."

—1 Kings 18:46 (NKJV)

The chariot was Ahab's *leverage*. But Elijah had God's supernatural catalyst. He outran horses and wheels, not by might, not by power, but by the Spirit of the Lord. That's divine empowerment.

Ruth: A Story of Catalyst and Leverage

Look at Ruth, chapter 3. When we first meet her, she is a widowed Moabite woman with no status, no provision, and no foreseeable future. But by the end of the chapter, everything has shifted. She is no longer begging in the fields. She is being redeemed, prepared, and positioned to become the wife of Boaz, a wealthy landowner and her kinsman-redeemer.

This shift didn't happen randomly. It happened because of both leverage and catalyst.

- Naomi was Ruth's leverage. Her proximity to Naomi positioned her to be in the right place at the right time. Naomi gave her detailed instructions on how to present herself, where to go, and how to prepare for her encounter with Boaz.

- God was Ruth's catalyst. While Naomi could get Ruth close to Boaz, only God could move Boaz's heart. Only God could cause the process to accelerate, and bring about a result that was faster and greater than human strategy alone could accomplish.

You may have mentors, coaches, tools, and strategies. These are your levers. But you must also believe that God is your catalyst. He can do in one day what would normally take ten years. He can make people notice you without you ever marketing yourself. He can breathe on your effort and turn it into an exponential impact.

I believe God was our catalyst when we needed a location to host our 3rd networking event. The year before, we did it outside. And while Elijah prayed for rain to come, we had to pray for it to stop. This year we decided to stay inside. The hall we rented was a result of God being our catalyst. We got it for a price no other place (even smaller in size) offered us.

Favor Will Accelerate You

I see and declare this over your life: quick results are coming to you. You are stepping into a season of divine acceleration—where the oil of ease flows over your work, and God's hand becomes unmistakable. The word prosperity and its root word "prosper" stems from the Hebrew word tsalach. One of the definitions is "ease."

It might be that you're just starting out in your business or ministry and feel like you're miles behind. But remember, a catalyst doesn't require you to be ahead—it simply requires you to be *yielded*.

Sometimes, it won't take years for the world to recognize your gift. Like a rising music artist who suddenly gets a collaboration with a well-known name, one moment of divine favor can shift your entire trajectory. That collaboration—*that* platform—can become your launching pad. And when God is behind it, no one can take the credit but Him.

Final Charge: Build With God, For God

So whether it's a product you're launching, a platform you're building, or a purpose you're pursuing—*remember*

Whose business it is. Ask God for both leverage and catalytic favor. Ask Him to bring the right people, the right tools, the right strategies into your life, but also to breathe on it with supernatural acceleration.

Because when it's God's business, He supplies the favor. And with favor comes both the leverage and the catalyst to go farther and faster, with His name lifted high.

15

The Well

The Bible is full of moments when God's provision shows up; sometimes suddenly, and other times, it had been right there all along. Over and over again, Scripture paints the picture of a loving Father who provides for His people, especially those who turn to Him in faith. One of the most powerful symbols of God's provision is **the well**: a hidden, deep, sustaining source of life, often revealed in a moment of desperation.

A Story of Despair

Take Hagar, for example. A name that doesn't often headline sermons, yet her story holds profound insight for anyone who's ever felt abandoned, used, or left with "not enough." Hagar was Sarah's servant. When Sarah couldn't conceive, she offered Hagar to Abraham as a "fill in." The plan was for Hagar to have Abraham's child. Predictably, the situation turned toxic. Years later, after Sarah gave birth to Isaac, jealousy took over. Hagar and her son Ishmael were sent away into the wilderness, armed with only a bottle of water and a loaf of bread.

The Bible says that when the water was gone, Hagar placed her child under a bush and walked a short distance away, saying, "I cannot watch the boy die." It's hard to imagine the depth of her despair. She was a single mother, exiled, and facing death by starvation with her child in the middle of a barren wilderness.

But then **God stepped in**.

When Heaven Opens Our Eyes

In Genesis 21:17–19, it says that **God heard the boy crying**, and an angel of God called to Hagar, telling her not to be afraid. Then something extraordinary happened: *"God opened her eyes, and she saw a well of water."* She went, filled the skin, and gave her son a drink.

Some scholars believe the well was always there. Others argue that God miraculously provided it in that moment. But either way, the result is the same: her eyes were opened, and she was able to see what would save her and her son.

That image has never left me: **a woman in crisis, weeping over a dried-up bottle, while an entire well waited within reach.**

The Well in Business

How often do we find ourselves crying over "dried-up bottles" in business? Is it a failed product launch, or clients who somehow vanish? Is it that your revenue doesn't match the amount of effort you've been putting in? Are you facing the pressure of wearing every hat as a solo entrepreneur?

Like Hagar, we've all felt moments of utter depletion. Moments where the "math doesn't math", and our efforts seem to fall flat. But here's what I've learned in both Scripture and in real entrepreneurial life:

God always has a well.

He never leaves us to survive on scraps forever. What we need is not always *more hustle*. Sometimes, what we need is **clarity**, **vision**, and **spiritual sight**. Hagar didn't need a miracle as much as she needed **her eyes opened**. And I believe the same is true for us. There may already be a well (a strategy, connection, resource, or revelation) that God is waiting to reveal the moment we cry out to Him. This is why spending time in His presence as mentioned in the previous chapter is so important

There was another woman whose eyes God opened to the best well she would ever encounter. Just like this woman, there are many times in life that we think we are coming to draw from one source, only to realize that God has orchestrated the moment so *He* can pour into *us*. This was the case for the woman of Samaria. She came to the well like she did every day: carrying her past, her shame, her daily needs. But what she didn't realize was that **she was about to meet the Well Himself**.

A Divine Interruption

In John 4, Jesus takes a surprising route through Samaria; a place Jews normally avoided. He sits by a well, weary from travel, and waits for someone. It's around noon, a time when most women wouldn't be drawing water because of the heat. But then she comes: the Samaritan woman, alone. And Jesus says to her, *"Give me a drink."* This was more than a request for water. It was an invitation to conversation, to transformation. The woman is shocked that a Jewish man is speaking to her, a Samaritan woman with a complicated past. She had a number of previous husbands and was currently living with a man who wasn't her husband. In every way, she was a societal outcast. But Jesus wasn't there to judge her, He was there to **restore her**. He tells her in verses 13–14:

"Everyone who drinks this water will be thirsty again, but whoever drinks the water I give them will never thirst. Indeed, the water I give will become in them a spring of water welling up to eternal life."

In that moment, Jesus flips the entire script. She came to the well thinking she needed **water**. But Jesus reveals she needed **Living Water: Him**.

The Samaritan woman's encounter at the well mirrors what many of us go through in life and in business. We come to our old "wells" which are social media, platforms, clients, income streams; hoping they will quench our thirst for significance, purpose, success, or even survival. For a while, they might. But the truth is, these earthly wells run dry. They are circumstantial. They depend on the season. And if we're honest, they often leave us thirstier than before.

Jesus didn't just offer the Samaritan woman a better *method*, He offered Himself. **He was the well** she needed. And the moment she began to listen to Him, her eyes were opened. Her identity shifted. She dropped her water jar, ran into the city, and told everyone about this man who "told me everything I ever did." She became the very first evangelist to her community, all from one encounter.

It's easy to center our business on *strategy*, but not on *Savior*. To prioritize *hustle*, but not *Holy Spirit*. But when

Jesus becomes your well, **your business becomes more than a brand, it becomes a testimony. You'll notice some drastic changes. You won't be** operating from fear and you'll start building from faith. You won't be chasing validation but rather walking in authority.

Jesus told the woman, *"If you knew who it was who asked you..."* And I believe He's saying the same to us today. If we *really knew* the Source we have access to, we wouldn't be scrambling for likes, striving for relevance, or stressing over provision. We would be drawing from a *never-ending flow of wisdom, creativity, and strategy.* Can I emphasize "never-ending?"

He is the CEO. He is the investor. He is the board. He is the brand builder. When we let Him into the core of our business (not just our prayer time) He turns daily grind into divine impact.

Buckets and Bottles vs. Wells

A bottle or bucket represents **limited provision**, often man-made, short-term, and not meant to sustain. We cling to these in business when we overwork without wise systems, chase trends instead of vision, or rely on single income streams. But a **well**? A well is deep, and sustaining. It represents God's way. Wells aren't flashy. They often require digging. But once tapped, they flow with *abundance*. The question is: are you willing to stop staring at your bottle long enough to ask God to open your eyes to the well?

Isaac was another Bible character that God blessed abundantly with wells. He had many! However, his prosperity wasn't without resistance. As he reopened his father's wells and dug new ones, the Philistines quarreled with him over them (Genesis 26:18-21). They even blocked his wells. Still, Isaac didn't fight; he moved on and kept digging until he reached **Rehoboth**, saying,

"At last the Lord has created enough space for us to prosper in this land"

—Genesis 26:22, NLT.

Isaac's wealth wasn't just about what he gained, it was about how he kept moving forward and trusting God's provision with every well he dug.

Business Insight: Finding Your Well

Every business leader needs to ask: **Where is my well?**

- Is there a skill I've overlooked that can become a product or service?

- Is there a person I need to connect or reconnect with who holds a key to my next season?

- Is God calling me to shift my model, and I've been too afraid to move?

God doesn't just provide for our *spiritual* needs. He is also the **God of strategy**, the **God of innovation**, and the **God of systems**. When we commit our work to Him, He does more than bless it. He gives us eyes to see what was there all along: provisions, solutions and ideas.

El-Roi: The God Who Sees You

Hagar named God **El-Roi**, *"The God who sees me."* That wasn't just about her physical location; it was about her emotional state, her fears, her future. God saw all of it and responded with provision.

I pray the same for you in your business. I pray that you'll know Him as El-Roi. That when the resources look dry, He will open your eyes to the well. That you won't settle for bottles when God has called you to dig deep and drink from His endless supply.

God doesn't just see your business. He sees **you**. He cares. And He will provide.

Notice what happened when the Samaritan woman received Jesus:

- She left her water jar. (She no longer needed what she thought she came for.)

- She ran to tell others. (Boldness replaced shame.)

- She brought a harvest. (The entire town came to see Jesus because of her testimony.)

Let that speak to you. There is a shift that happens when Jesus becomes your well. You go from trying to draw life out of dry routines, to becoming a wellspring of living water for others. You go from barely showing up online to confidently showing up in purpose. You go from "I hope this works" to "I know who sent me."

When Jesus is your well, you become a well for others.

16

THE LAME MAN - GET YOUR POWER BACK

The Bible is filled with stories of miracles. There are so many mighty acts of healing, provision, deliverance, and breakthrough. From the prophets of the Old Testament to the apostles of the New, and especially through the ministry of Jesus, we see supernatural interventions in natural circumstances. But among all these miracles, there's one story that strikes a deep and personal chord with me. It's the story of the *impotent man* at the Pool of Bethesda.

I had the opportunity to visit Israel a couple of years back and I remember passing by the remains of the pool of Bethesda. Though we were there for only a few minutes, I couldn't help but get lost in imagining what it would have been like 2000 years ago. A place full of impotent people waiting for their change to come. A dreary place of sadness, and hopelessness.

Topically, Jesus healing the impotent man may not seem the most dramatic miracle. No Red Sea parts. No fire falls from heaven. But this miracle is relatable, raw, and real. Because while I've never had a physical walking disability, I've definitely felt spiritually, mentally, and emotionally *impotent*. Stuck. Paralyzed. Waiting on something to change.

Let's look at the story from John

"In these lay a great multitude of impotent folk, of blind, halt, withered, waiting for the moving of the water... And a certain man was there, which had an infirmity thirty and eight years. When Jesus saw him lie, and knew that he had been now a long time in that case, he saith unto him, ***Wilt thou be made whole?*** *The impotent man answered him, Sir, I have no man, when the water is troubled, to put me into the pool... Jesus saith unto him,* ***Rise, take up thy bed, and walk.****"*

—John 5:2–9 (KJV)

Impotent: Powerless in a Place of Waiting

The Bible describes the people at Bethesda with specific conditions: impotent, blind, halt, and withered. All of them were waiting **for something outside of themselves to stir change.** The word "impotent" stood out to me.

If God is *omnipotent*—all-powerful—then impotent must mean the opposite: lacking power.

In the Greek, the word *akratēs* means **powerless, weak, poor, and needy**. Sound familiar? It describes more than physical sickness. It describes a mindset, a spiritual condition, and for many of us in the realm of business, it describes a cycle.

Poverty is a system of impotency. It's not just about the lack of money, but about the lack of **movement**. It's the lack of the growth mindset, lack of strategy, and lack of vision. We know we're called to build, lead, and create, but we stay stuck waiting for the "right conditions." Waiting for someone to sponsor us. Waiting for the perfect moment. Waiting for someone to give us permission. All the while, the years are passing.

Just like the man at the pool, we find ourselves surrounded by other "impotent folk." There's a quote by Jim Rohn: *"You are the average of the five people you spend the most time with."* If you're surrounded by people who are stuck, broke, excuse-driven, or fearful, it becomes your normal. Your mind adjusts to the environment and begins to mirror it.

Bethesda wasn't just a place. It was a **culture of waiting.** A gathering place for stuck people.

What Are You Focused On?

When Jesus comes to the man, He asks a powerful, but simple question: **"Wilt thou be made whole?"** In other words, *do you actually want to be free?*

And the man's answer is an excuse. *"I have no man to help me..."* It's subtle, but so real. Instead of saying "Yes!" the man explains why he can't be healed. His focus is still on the pool. On the old way. On what he thought was the only option for change.

This is how many of us show up in business. We say we want breakthroughs. We say we want financial freedom. We pray for expansion. But when God sends an idea, a mentor, a course, a divine connection, we give Him an excuse: *"I don't have money... I don't know where to start... No one in my family has ever done this before... I need someone to help me first."*

Meanwhile, Jesus never even mentioned the pool. Because **He had something better in mind.**

When I attended my first business conference alone, I felt like God was giving me the opportunity to be "made whole." I was so used to going with a few friends who had and still have aspirations of becoming an entrepreneur. But this time, they weren't able to go. I wanted to cower in fear. I wanted to hide behind so many excuses for me not to go. But God asked me the question, "Do you want to be free?" I knew that something had to break. Something had to change and sometimes it requires going alone. Needless to say, the conference was exactly what I needed to pull from for building the business to grow that season. It set some foundational values that we needed to steady the business on.

We often want the *pool*, but Jesus wants to give us *power*. The man had been so fixated on one way of getting free that he couldn't recognize that Freedom Himself was standing in front of him.

We Don't Need a Pool When We Have a Word

For 38 years, this man had a single plan. A single strategy. A single way of thinking. And it never worked. He stayed paralyzed at the edge of what he thought was his breakthrough, never realizing that God could bypass the system entirely.

Some of us are standing by our own "pools." We are waiting for things to be perfect before we move, when Jesus is offering us a *word* that activates our destiny. A single instruction that shifts everything: *"Rise, take up your bed, and walk."*

Take up your bed! The thing that held you down in your oppression. You are above! Take it up and walk in faith so that your breakthrough comes. In your business, God is calling you to move; not when things change, but **so things can change.** You don't need more motivation. You need movement. You don't need to wait for someone to pull you in. You need to stand up. Sometimes the miracle isn't in the water. It's in the **obedience.**

More Than the Blessing

The man just wanted healing. But Jesus gave him **wholeness.**

He didn't just walk away from that pool physically restored. He walked away wholly restored. With a story of divine intervention. With a new identity.

We often ask God for the blessing we can see, but God wants to give us **wholeness**. With wholeness first, everything else starts flowing: income, influence, increase, strategy, and peace. The kind of blessing that doesn't just elevate our life, but transforms the lives of others through us.

Final Thoughts

You are not impotent. You are not stuck. You are not forgotten. You are not too late.

What's holding you back isn't your skill, your background, or your bank account. It's the belief that you need a pool to be healed. That your breakthrough must come in the way you imagined.

But God is doing a **new thing**. He's walking into your Bethesda (the place where others gave up) and calling you to rise.

In business and in life, stop staring at the water. Listen for the word.

17

STRETCH YOUR TENT - CULTIVATING THE GROWTH MINDSET

The Principle of Capacity

It's safe to say that everyone desires growth personally, spiritually, and professionally. In entrepreneurship, especially for start-ups and new business owners, growth is the goal. We set revenue targets, marketing goals, and expansion plans, expecting results within a specific time frame. But let's be honest, nothing truly meaningful happens overnight. Scripture reminds us that wealth that comes too quickly may not last, but gradual growth builds stability:

"Wealth from get-rich-quick schemes quickly disappears; wealth from hard work grows over time."

—Proverbs 13:11, NLT

Growth is a process, but more importantly, it's a process that requires preparation. You must create space for what you're asking God to send. Without the capacity to hold the blessing, it could either break you or pass you by altogether.

Isaiah: The Call to Enlarge

In Isaiah 54, we find a powerful metaphor that speaks directly to the idea of capacity:

"Enlarge your house; build an addition. Spread out your home, and spare no expense! For you will soon be bursting at the seams. Your descendants will occupy other nations and resettle the ruined cities."

—Isaiah 54:2–3, NLT

In this passage, God speaks to a barren woman (symbolic of Israel) who had been unfruitful and humiliated. But God promises a future of fruitfulness and expansion. The interesting part is the order of instruction: *Enlarge first, then expect.*

Before there was a visible blessing, before there was a child or a harvest, God gave a directive: *"Make room."* Why? Because blessings require space.

In business, this is critical. If you're praying for more clients, but you have no onboarding system, no website, no automated email funnel, are you really ready? If you're asking God to expand your brand, but you're still operating like a hobbyist instead of a CEO, can you handle the growth you're requesting? Capacity is ugly sometimes. It looks like sleepless nights, it looks like missing out on things you love.

God doesn't waste miracles. He often waits until there's a structure that can support the blessing. And in some cases, He won't send the increase until you've proven that you've made space for it.

Luke 5: The NET vs. NETS Problem

Now let's take a look at Peter, the fisherman, in Luke 5. After a long, unproductive night of fishing, Jesus tells Peter:

"Now go out where it is deeper, and let down your nets to catch some fish."

—Luke 5:4, NLT

But what does Peter do?

"Master," Simon replied, "we worked hard all last night and didn't catch a thing. But if you say so, I'll let the net down again."

—Luke 5:5, NLT

Jesus said "nets" (plural), but Peter responded with "net" (singular). The result?

"And this time their nets were so full of fish they began to tear! A shout for help brought their partners in the other boat, and soon both boats were filled with fish and on the verge of sinking."

—Luke 5:6–7, NLT

Peter obeyed but not fully. And that partial obedience led to broken nets and sinking boats. He wasn't prepared for the abundance. This is the danger of limited capacity. God wants to bless us immeasurably but He also wants to see if we've built the infrastructure to contain it. Imagine the "sea" as the marketplace. It's volatile—up and down. But if Jesus is telling you to throw out the nets into the sea for a catch that means that when you "launch out" again you'll be sure to be blessed.

Think of "launching out" as launching that new business or book. Think about launching as trying that business plan one more time now that Jesus is in your boat.

Imagine how many fish Peter didn't catch that day simply because his *net broke*. Similarly, in your business, what opportunities could you be missing because your systems are not prepared? Because your mindset is not stretched enough? Because your confidence, character, or capacity hasn't caught up with your vision?

Practical Ways to Build Capacity in Business

Building capacity isn't just spiritual, it's strategic. It's not about overworking or overreaching, but about intentionally preparing for what's in store. Here are a few ways to build capacity in your business:

1. Say NO More Often Saying "no" to distractions or draining opportunities gives you the mental bandwidth to focus on what matters most. Growth often comes from focus, not scattered effort.

2. Invest in Infrastructure If you've been running your business from your kitchen table, maybe it's time to invest in a dedicated office space or virtual assistant. Making a faith move to expand your workspace could be the very thing that signals to God, "I'm ready for more."

3. Clear Your Schedule Eliminate time-wasters. Delegate what you can. Free up your hours for what moves the needle. If you're called to build something impactful, your calendar should reflect your calling.

4. Stretch Strategically Growth will always require a stretch mentally, spiritually, and/or physically. Stretching isn't always comfortable but it helps your experience more blessings. Be comfortable with being uncomfortable. If you're trying to read more, challenge yourself to read a book a month. If you want to speak better, practice by posting consistently online. Imagine if the one net that Peter launched was small in size. He would've caught less and lost more than what he did. So stretch that net.

The Three C's: Confidence, Character, Capacity

When I created the *Find Your Voice Intensive*, the third module was all about building the *Three C's*:

Confidence, Character, and Capacity.

If you want to find your "voice"/purpose, you must be confident in the God that called you and in yourself. If you want to be trusted by God with your purpose, He has to be able to trust your character. But the last one is what will sustain your journey in fulfilling your purpose: building capacity.

God will never call you to a level that He hasn't equipped you to handle. But the equipping often begins with your decision to *enlarge your tent*. Before He fills, He wants to see you build.

"If you are faithful in little things, you will be faithful in large ones."

—Luke 16:10a, NLT

Elisha: Leaving Comfort to Catch Capacity

Another powerful example of building capacity and leading with a growth mindset is found in the relationship between Elisha and his mentor Elijah. When Elijah came to call Elisha, the young man was in a comfortable and stable position; working the family business, plowing the fields with twelve teams of oxen. But when Elijah threw his cloak over Elisha (a symbolic act of calling) Elisha knew everything had to change.

"Elijah went over to him and threw his cloak across his shoulders and then walked away. Elisha left the oxen standing there, ran after Elijah, and said to him, 'First let me go and kiss my father and mother good-bye, and then I will go with you!'"

—1 Kings 19:19–20, NLT

Elisha didn't just leave his work. He destroyed the plow, sacrificed the oxen, and fed the people. That was a permanent decision to not return to the old way. He burned the bridge to comfort so he could fully embrace his calling. That is a clear representation of what it means to have a growth mindset. Later, when Elijah was taken up to heaven, Elisha was the only one close enough and "prepared enough" to receive the mantle.

"Elisha picked up Elijah's cloak, which had fallen when he was taken up. Then Elisha returned to the bank of the Jordan River."

—2 Kings 2:13, NLT

Elisha's capacity grew not just because of his proximity to Elijah, but because of his willingness to *leave* what was familiar. In business and in life, there will be times when comfort becomes the enemy of capacity. You may have to walk away from good to step into *God*. You may need to release what's stable to receive what's supernatural.

The Growth Mindset and Capacity

Building capacity starts in the mind. A growth mindset is the belief that your abilities, business, and spiritual influence can expand with effort and intention. This is essential. Without it, you'll reject challenges that are actually divine invitations to stretch. A fixed mindset keeps you safe; a growth mindset positions you for overflow. When you believe that God can do more through you, you'll prepare differently, you'll build differently, and you'll lead differently. Capacity begins where belief expands.

It's easy to say "God is about to bless me!" based on Malachi 3:10:

"I will pour out a blessing so great you won't have enough room to take it in! Try it! Put me to the test!"

—Malachi 3:10b, NLT

But that promise was given to people who first obeyed the principle of giving. God *responds* to our preparation.

So, what does building capacity look like for you right now? What system, mindset, or environment needs expansion? You don't want to receive a blessing that you aren't ready to sustain. Stretch. Prepare. Build. Make room before the rain.

18

THE 9 LAWS OF GIANT SUCCESS

If you want to achieve the highest level of success in business while growing according to God's way, then you need to understand and apply these nine LAWS for GIANT Success: principles that have been exemplified by nine of some of the greatest giants in the Bible, each of whom dominated their mountain of influence. These are not just helpful suggestions; they are **non-negotiable laws** that you **must** follow in order to experience God's abundance and fulfill your divine purpose. In physics, for a principle to be considered a law, it must consistently produce the same results when applied under the same conditions. Likewise, I firmly believe that when we align our lives with the timeless, God-ordained principles modeled by these biblical giants, we position ourselves for **predictable, supernatural results**; the kind that lead to true, lasting success. These are the 9 laws: **Knowing God,**

Qavah, Faith, Diligence, Resoluteness, Prudence, Humility, Declaration, and Decreeing

The Law of Knowing Your God

Those who truly **know** their God are strong and do great exploits. This is a powerful truth we learn from the life of Daniel. He is one of my favorite biblical figures, and for good reason. The Bible tells us that a **spirit of excellence** rested upon him, allowing him to transcend the reigns of four to five different kings while maintaining his position as a trusted advisor and prince. What made Daniel exceptional was his ability to meet the standards of these earthly rulers **without ever compromising the standards of God Almighty**.

Time and time again, his integrity was tested, yet he remained unshaken. One of the most memorable examples of this is when the wicked princes, jealous of his favor, tricked the king into signing a decree that forbade prayer to anyone except the king himself. But Daniel, who was fully committed to the law of knowing God, continued to pray, risking his very life. The Hebrew word for "know" signifies **deep intimacy**, and Daniel understood that the most powerful way to cultivate intimacy with God was through prayer. This law wasn't just a principle he followed. It was the very foundation of his life. It sustained him in positions of influence and, more importantly, sustained him in the lion's den. Because he knew his God, he was unshakable, and ultimately, **untouchable**. This essentially was how Daniel maintained the spirit of excellence.

How can you apply this principle? By spending time in the word of God. You also can spend intentional time praying and pressing into His presence. That's honestly where inspiration comes for all of my ideas for products and services. That's certainly where I got the inspiration for this book. When you Know your God, you will do exploits

The Law of Qavah

The Bible tells us that the children of Israel were under severe oppression for 20 years. They disobeyed God and were captured by king Jabin of the Canaanites. An evil man named Sisera was the commander of the army. But then one day, Deborah the judge of Israel rose up! Twenty years of oppression over in one day. How? Deborah's secret was what I like to call " the law of Qavah". Qavah is one of the many Hebrew words that means to dwell, remain, sit, abide, wait. But it's not a passive kind of waiting. You wait with expectancy, with hope, that your Father will answer. It means to sit until God does something.

Deborah understood the power of **dwelling** in God's presence. It's in the **staying** that true empowerment comes. Deborah **lived** in God's presence. The Bible tells us that she dwelled between **Bethel** and **Ramah**, meaning **"the house of God"** and **"the high place"**. Her consistent communion with God positioned her to receive divine wisdom, and clarity, that could only come from Him.

Many people run into prayer expecting God to answer in 10 seconds, but do we have the power to wait on Him for instructions? Deborah knew that the only way she would come up with God's divine plan to free the Israelites was if she waited on Him. That was the strategy.

Business owners, CEO's Leaders in the making, hear me when I say that the best thing you can learn to do is Qavah on God. It brings forth a MASSIVE breakthrough.

The Law of Faith

But without faith it is impossible to please him*: for he that cometh to God must believe that he is, and that he is a rewarder of them that diligently seek him.*

—Hebrews 11:6 KJV

Who better to talk about concerning faith than the father of faith himself—Abraham? He was the perfect example of what it looked like to walk with God even when you don't know what the next step looks like. For all leaders, entrepreneurs and believers in general, I want you to lean all the way in. You are going to come into seasons in your life where you will feel blindfolded. All you'll have to hold on to in the hand of Jesus and the belief that He will take you safely through the journey.

If you are building a business, especially one that you are pioneering, it will get hard. But engaging the law of faith will bring you from vision to reality.

Abraham was one hundred years old when Isaac the promise child was born. Even after Isaac was born, Abraham's faith was tested. God told him to sacrifice the child he had waited over 20 years for. Not only had he waited, but his wife waited, suffered shame, and fear that she would never have her promised child. The journey to

Mount Moriah (the place he would carry out the sacrifice was a three day journey. Three days to think long and hard about changing his mind. But Abraham's faith was so strong in God, that even when Isaac--ignorant to what was about to happen--asked him where the sacrifice was, Abraham answered that God would provide the sacrifice. And indeed, God provided the sacrifice. That's where we see another dimension of God, *Jehovah Jireh*--A place in your life where God will provide.

The Law of Humility

The Bible tells us that Moses was **the most meek (humble) man** to ever walk the earth. His humility wasn't just a personality trait, but a posture of the heart that made him a vessel for **great exploits**. Moses didn't seek power, yet God entrusted him with **leading an entire nation** through the wilderness for 40 years. His heart was so burdened for the people that he willingly carried their struggles, interceded for them, and even pleaded with God on their behalf. Though Moses' level of humility might have seemed like weakness, it was actually **the key to his authority and leadership**.

Humility has the power to open doors you never imagined walking through. When God commanded Moses to go before Pharaoh, there was no grand preparation, no years of training. He was just given an assignment and took a step of obedience. Even then, Moses hesitated, insisting that his brother Aaron take the lead. But God refused. Why? Because Moses wasn't chosen for his eloquence or confidence. Moses was chosen and set apart because of his willingness to **submit himself fully to God's power**, even when he felt unqualified.

Moses was more than a leader. In my opinion, he exhibited the perfect example of what a modern day pastor should be like. He continuously sought God's face on behalf of others. His story teaches us that true humility isn't thinking less of yourself. It's thinking of **God's power** more. And when you walk in that kind of humility, God will elevate you to places you never thought possible.

Moses was willing to deny himself food sometimes, and the pleasure of his family to constantly seek God's heart on how to lead these people. He was willing to bear their load on his shoulders before his father in law taught him how to delegate. The fact that he took the advice of his father in law shows humility. Well advised. The book of Proverbs tells us that the inverse of well-advised people are foolish people.

Even after performing 10 plagues of Egypt and parting the RED SEA for thousands of people to cross safely and for the enemies to drown, Moses NEVER glorified himself. Do you see the pattern? Can you see the law at work? Moses exercised this law of humility and it made him a successful leader.

Even though He didn't make it to the promised land, Moses was seen on the mount of Transfiguration and mentioned in the Hall of Faith in Hebrews chapter 11. Can God trust you to walk in humility if He gave you the influence over thousands of people? Can He trust you not to take any glory if He uses your anointing and platform to bring people to Him? Can He trust you to let your light shine so people can **see your good works** and **glorify Him**? We have to always remember that it's all about Him. When we tell people about Christ and they come to him, No glory should ever go to us, but first to God. THEN He will reward us.

Are you willing to let God work on you daily? We have to be nurtured and formed into the image of Christ day by day. Humility takes work! It takes self denial, and seeing God and His purpose for your life bigger than you see yourself. Scripture tells us that our spirit man must be renewed everyday. It can only be renewed by staying connected to the source that replenishes and refines it. The refiner's fire is HOT! So while the refinement part doesn't feel good, God replenishes us through people and through His word.

Humble yourselves therefore under the mighty hand of God, that he may exalt you in due time

—1 Peter 5:6

The Law of Diligence

"A slack hand causes poverty, but the hand of the diligent makes rich. He who gathers in summer is a prudent son, but he who sleeps in harvest is a son who brings shame."

— Proverbs 10:4-5 (ESV)

Diligence is the ability to work without anyone pushing you to do so. There is a natural drive. Ruth is the perfect personification of engaging the law of diligence. This scripture from proverbs is a verse Ruth would probably have resonated with. When she and Naomi moved back to Bethlehem (house of bread) she knew that the "bread" wouldn't just fall in her lap. She would have to work for it. Ruth decided to find a field to glean in. So in the terms of Proverbs 10:4-5, her hands were not slack. Because of her diligence, she was made rich in not only grain, but in security, love and redemption.

The Law of Resilience & Resoluteness

1 Corinthians 16:9 Paul updates the Corinthians on his status, where he is staying and where he plans on staying next. He says something that is worth paying attention to. **THERE IS A GREAT DOOR** opened for me, EFFECTUAL, But I am being resisted:

For a great door and effectual is opened unto me, and there are many adversaries.

— 1 Corinthians 16:9 (KJV)

In verse 8, Paul speaks about staying in Ephesus *because* the door is open and resistance is great. Whenever God has work for you to do, the greater the door, the greater the opposition. You're going to need resilience in business, ministry, governmental work, education, or just about any mountain you are attaining. Passion is needed, but grit is as well. When life and dark forces begin to push you back, resoluteness and resilience is what keeps your feet from slipping.

The Law of Prudence

Joseph was a man of prudence. When he was given the authority to be keeper of his master Potiphar's house, he worked tirelessly to keep everything in order. One day, Potiphar's wife came to him, tempting him to sleep with her. His answer was a clear statement of prudence and integrity:

How can I do this wicked thing and sin against my God?

Though his integrity and prudence cost him his job, God honored him and put him in a position far higher than Potiphar's house. Prudence is the ability to make just and sober decisions for a better future. It's the ability to ignore instant gratification of speaking back, spending erroneously, or making decisions on a whim; considering the decision best for a more honorable outcome.

There will be times where you will be tested. You might be tempted to take an unfair deal. You might be tempted to tell lies in order to sign a contract. What will your resolve be? Choose prudence.

The Law of Declarations

This is one of my favorite laws by far. Declaring is a way to partner with God. Decreeing and declaring are similar, but have significant differences that we will go over. The law of declaring gives you the advantage as a believer, to enforce what God said, and fight the powers of the enemy. Words carry life and death. All the devil needs to do is use someone or something to declare the opposite of what God says. All he needs *you* to do is come into agreement with him.

In 1 Kings 18 after God kills all of the false prophets on the mount of Carmel, Elijah hears from God that there is the sound of an abundance of rain. God showed Elijah that this rain would be such a heavy downpour to reverse the drought they experienced. He believed it so much that He told king Ahab to celebrate! But even while he told him to celebrate, Elijah went back to Mount Carmel to enforce what God said about the rain. The Bible says he "cast his head between his knees" and began to pray. It was a fervent prayer. While he was there, He kept sending his servant to look for evidence of what he heard. Everytime the servant came back and said there was no cloud, Elijah prayed again. All Elijah was doing here was declaring and enforcing in the earth realm, what God already said in the spirit realm. Eventually his servant saw a cloud the size of a man's hands. Had Elijah given up and said "You know what, forget it, there's no rain coming", maybe he would have missed his opportunity to partner with God.

And Elijah said unto Ahab, Get thee up, eat and drink; for there is a sound of abundance of rain. So Ahab went up to eat and to drink. And Elijah went up to the top of Carmel; and he cast himself down upon the earth, and put his face between his knees, And said to his servant, Go up now, look toward the sea. And he went up, and looked, and said, There is nothing. And he said, Go again seven times. And it came to pass at the seventh time, that he said, Behold, there ariseth a little cloud out of the sea, like a man's hand. And he said, Go up, say unto Ahab, Prepare thy chariot, and get thee down, that the rain stop thee not

— 1 Kings 18:41-44 (KJV)

The Hebrew definition of declare means "to set forth". Even though God says it, you can partner with Him, to set it forth. Begin to declare over your family, your health, your finances, and your business, whatever God's word says about those things. If you don't know what to declare, the word is the BEST declaration.

The Law of Decrees

Biblical kings understood that whenever they wrote decrees, they typically couldn't revoke it even if they wanted to. Once the decree was made and the decree had the seal on it, it had to be enforced. They would just have to make a stronger decree to revert the old one if they wanted to change it. We see this in the story of Daniel. There was a set up against Daniel to kill him. The king was tricked into signing a decree that anyone who worships another god or thing, other than the king, they must be thrown in the lion's den.

The king was distraught once he found out the decree would have killed Daniel; he regretted it instantly. He wouldn't eat. He wouldn't drink because it was written and therefore could not be revoked. We know that the favor of God was with Daniel however, and he was safe in the lion's den.

After Daniel was set free from the lion's den and those who set him up were eaten by the lions, the king made a new decree to avert the old one. Something similar happened where King Xerxes in the book of Esther, wrote a decree when tricked by Haman to destroy all the jews.

In the natural world, it seems as though another decree being written was what saved Daniel, Esther and her people. But the true secret key that revoked those written decrees, were the ones Daniel and Esther released while they were waiting. I can just imagine Daniel looking at those lions, praying and decreeing that God would shut their mouths.

I can just imagine Esther in her time of praying and fasting, how she would walk up and down within the palace walls, disseminating decrees in the realm of the spirit. She cried out to God for help, and those decrees for her death and her people were revoked. Even though decrees could not physically be revoked—only replaced with a higher decree—in the spirit, God canceled it.

Begin to decree that you are the head and not the tail. Decree that your business shall flourish as long as it aligns with the will of the Father. Whenever you hit a roadblock and things don't seem to be working smoothly, begin to decree the word of God over it. Speak life, even when you feel hopeless. If you genuinely don't have the strength, ask God to send people who will decree over you.

I hope these 9 laws will bring tremendous transformation to your life. May God show up in unique ways and cause your business to flourish.

Pay attention and turn your ear to the sayings of the wise; apply your heart to what I teach, for it is pleasing when you keep them in your heart

and have all of them ready on your lips. So that your trust may be in the Lord, I teach you today, even you.

-- Proverbs 22:17-19

19

THE JOURNEY, THE SOJOURNER, AND THE ROADMAP

One January morning, I sat outside on my porch in sandals, a linen top, and a flowing maxi skirt. The sun blazed overhead, and my sunglasses sat perched atop my head. I had just come back inside, shielding my eyes from the radiant Mexican sun, stunned by what I had just heard. My mouth was wide open.

There I was, on a solo weekend trip in Mexico, seeking God for strategy and instruction for our business in 2025. I hadn't known exactly what to expect, but I knew I was supposed to go. God had instructed me to get still, get away, and prepare to hear from Him. A few weeks earlier, I'd signed up for a free business strategy session from an Instagram ad. I didn't think much of it at the time and had completely forgotten about it—until that morning, when I came in from breakfast and saw the live session email.

I decided to click in. That one click changed the entire trajectory of my year.

Dean Graziosi was teaching on the *12 Keys to Business Success*. Every word he spoke felt divinely timed, as though heaven had sent a kiss on my cheek. After my connecting flight had been canceled—only for me to be rebooked in first class straight to Mexico—I already felt God's favor. But then came Dean's words:

"What if you had a roadmap that could lead you across your field of obstacles 10x quicker? Would you take the roadmap—or would you choose to go it alone?"

That question pierced me. He was talking about mentorship—having someone who's already walked the road ahead and is now handing you a guide. Not so you can avoid every bump, but so you can move forward with wisdom, insight, and acceleration.

Gleaning vs. Mentorship

In the last chapter, we talked about gleaning: gathering wisdom from people you encounter in everyday life. A customer at your job, a social media leader, or a neighbor who shares stories that stick. Gleaning is powerful, but mentorship is a whole other dimension. It's not random. It's intentional.

Mentorship is about journeying with a sojourner who has gone before you and knows the terrain.

The Biblical Blueprint: Elijah and Elisha

The story of Elijah and Elisha is one of the clearest examples in Scripture of the power of mentorship. Elijah was a prophet who endured great hardship. He was a man of God whose journey was marked by intense warfare, divine intervention, isolation, and breakthrough. His office was weighty and costly. But in the midst of his journey, God gave him an assignment—to mentor Elisha, the one who would walk in his footsteps and, ultimately, have double the impact.

Elijah's journey became Elisha's roadmap.

Elijah performed **eight recorded miracles**, including:

- Shutting the heavens with a word, causing a three-and-a-half-year drought

- Multiplying flour and oil for a widow

- Raising a widow's son from the dead

- Calling down fire from heaven on Mount Carmel

- Parting the Jordan River

- Calling down fire on soldiers

Elisha, his spiritual son and mentee, went on to perform **sixteen miracles—exactly double**:

- Parted the Jordan River

- Healed poisoned waters in Jericho

- Provided miraculous oil for a widow

- Raised the Shunammite woman's son

- Multiplied food

- Healed Naaman of leprosy

And more...

What does this teach us? That mentorship not only transfers knowledge, it accelerates your journey. Elisha didn't just admire Elijah; he followed him closely, honored him, served him, and received the mantle when Elijah ascended. As a result, he was positioned to go further, faster.

Mentorship in Business: A Necessary Strategy

In business, a mentor is like that sojourner who's already navigated the land you're now entering. They've seen the pitfalls, the terrain changes, the industry shifts. They know the rise and fall of the climate. Learning from them doesn't mean you'll avoid all challenges, but it does mean you won't face them blindly.

Sometimes, your mentor is right in front of you. It could be a manager at your job. If you're still working in a corporate setting while nurturing your entrepreneurial dreams, consider this: you're getting paid to learn. Watch how your manager leads. Observe how they handle pressure, lead teams, and execute strategy. Ask questions. Offer help beyond your job description. Show leadership even before you hold the title. Why? Because honor and humility attract impartation.

A mentor could also be a spiritual leader, a community elder, or even someone you've never met personally but follow closely online. But here's the key: **mentors won't always be easily accessible**. Don't be offended if they don't respond the way you hoped. Pride and offense are dream killers. They block the flow of wisdom God is trying to get to you.

Coaching: The Accelerated Roadmap

Mentorship can be informal and observational. Coaching, however, is personal, direct, and often paid. A coach gives you access to their journey, tools, and systems with intentional focus on your specific goals. When you invest in a coach, you're not just buying information, you're buying acceleration.

Let's say you want to grow in etiquette and grace. You could try to figure it out on your own, or you could pay someone who has already mastered that area and created a clear system for transformation. The latter gets you results faster, with less trial and error.

It's the same in business. Want to build a profitable brand? Launch a digital product? Scale your services? Hire a coach who has done it and has a proven roadmap.

As entrepreneurs we must remember: **God often answers our prayers in the form of people.** Your next level is often hidden inside a conversation, a coaching program, a lunch meeting, or a mentorship moment.

Final Thoughts: Don't Walk Alone

You were never meant to walk this journey alone. The path to purpose is too rich to explore without guidance. Whether through mentors or coaches, your growth will be faster, wiser, and more impactful when you learn from those who've already journeyed through the terrain.

Just like Elisha, when you honor the mentor and receive the mantle, you're positioned for double: double wisdom, double favor, double results.

So here's your challenge: **Who is your Elijah? Whose field are you gleaning in? Who are you watching, serving, honoring, or investing in to help you on your journey?**

Because the truth is, every sojourner needs a roadmap. And mentorship is the map that makes the journey lighter and the destination closer.

20

Vision Is The Anchor

In the unpredictable seas of entrepreneurship, your vision is your anchor. It grounds you when the winds of uncertainty howl, when the waves of doubt rise, and when the storms of adversity threaten to overturn everything you've built. Without an anchor, a boat is left at the mercy of the storm, tossed about by the waves until it is lost. Without a vision, a business suffers the same fate: wandering, unstable, and eventually perishing.

The Bible tells us, *"Where there is no vision, the people perish"* (Proverbs 29:18). This truth applies not only to individuals and nations but also to businesses. Without a clear, unwavering vision, your business will lack direction, focus, and the endurance to withstand trials. It is not a question of *if* storms will come in entrepreneurship but *when*. And when they do, your vision must be strong enough to anchor you through them.

Lessons from Acts 27

In *Acts 27*, we find Paul and a group of men traveling by sea when, suddenly, a violent storm catches them off guard. For over two weeks, they are battered by fierce winds and raging waves (v. 33). The storm is so intense that the sailors (men trained to handle the sea) become overwhelmed with fear. Their instinct is to abandon ship. Verse 30 tells us, *"Then the sailors tried to abandon the ship; they lowered the lifeboat as though they were going to put out anchors from the front of the ship"* (NLT). Instead of securing the very thing that could stabilize them, they prepare to jump ship.

Have you ever been there? So frustrated with the storms of life and entrepreneurship that you just want to walk away? You've poured everything into your business—your time, energy, resources, and faith—only to be met with unforeseen struggles. Maybe sales have slowed, a major contract fell through, or unexpected challenges have drained your enthusiasm. You wonder, *Did I miss God? Should I just quit?*

Paul's response to the sailors is a word for you today: **"Stay on board and no lives will be lost."** If you're on the verge of giving up, I urge you, **don't jump ship!** God is depending on you to carry His precious cargo to its intended destination. Your business is not just a business;

it is an assignment. It is a vehicle for impact, provision, and legacy. The vision God gave you wasn't just for a season, it was for a purpose. When the winds get boisterous, don't forget the *why*.

In 2024 when we were planning our 2nd networking event, God shifted the theme and direction of the event from the year before. We were having a panel discussion on entrepreneurship from a faith perspective, and I knew exactly who I wanted to speak. We invited someone from out of the country to come. Everything felt like it was lining up perfectly. Until the day of the event. Those that were there that day, would know exactly what I'm talking about. The weather took a complete turn! We were doing the event outdoors and we prayed for the best. It was so sunny and hot all day, and then an hour before the event, the winds started blowing. It got dark. As we were preparing, people were calling me and asking if we were still doing the event. My husband and his friends were setting up the sound system and music for the night. Our TPE team was setting up the tables for vendors. We got a call that the winds were blowing hard. Then the ride for our special guest was trying to call her and couldn't get through. The winds and storms were so boisterous that the hotel she was staying at lost power! Can you believe it? That shows how bad it was. But in the midst of it all, the Holy Spirit kept me calm. He sent one of our team members to begin praying over me, Tenoy, and over the event. When we got to the site, people were coming in looking at me and Tenoy trying to read our faces. "Were we concerned? Were we going to cancel? Were we upset?" I remember going over to my husband and asking him what were we going to do next. He looked at me and said "What do you mean? Everything is set up already. There's no turning back."

At that moment, I had to let out my anchor. The storm in my mind was pushing me back and forth. But I called on the strength of God and let down my *vision*. I had to remember the WHY for all of this and keep that at the forefront. That's when I grabbed the mic and asked all those that were there to pray with me. I don't remember everything I said, but I remember vividly saying "I don't think God brought us all here just to be washed by the rain." As we started to pray, the rain poured even harder. But I remember us praying even harder, and before we knew it, the rain stopped. We looked in the sky and saw a double rainbow. God allowed the rain to stop and allowed us to have an amazing night full of fun, laughter, business education and empowerment. I also found out the following morning that there was actually a tornado that was passing through our city. While the event was going on and the rain stopped, I was getting calls of people's chairs being torn on their porches. I even found out that trees and street lines came down. BUT IN THE MIDST OF THAT, God held back the storm! Do not doubt the power of God and the power of prayer. But even more important to this chapter, don't forget your "WHY." Had I forgotten the "why" of the event, we would have packed up everything and went home. People that flew in and drove in from other states would have left feeling as if they wasted their time.

No successful entrepreneur has ever built something great without encountering resistance. The winds of financial setbacks, self-doubt, slow sales, shifting markets, and unexpected obstacles will blow against you. Let's even address the elephant in the room; there will be moments when you question whether you should continue this journey. There will even be moments when everything in you wants to abandon ship. But here's the truth: The presence of storms does not mean you are *failing*. It means you are *sailing*. No one encounters resistance standing still. It is only those who move forward that feel the force of the wind. And that is why your vision must be firmly in place; it keeps you from being tossed by every difficulty, every distraction, and every delay.

Revisiting the Vision in the Midst of the Storm

When the storm intensifies, you don't abandon the anchor; **you let it down deeper**. In the same way, when the trials of business become overwhelming, you must revisit your vision and remind yourself *why* you started. Here are some questions you and your team can ask yourselves:

- Why did you launch this business?

- What problem are you solving?

- Who are you serving?

- What impact are you making?

Your vision is not just a statement you write once and forget; it is a living, breathing value that must be revisited, reexamined, and reaffirmed. If your business is struggling, don't just react to the storm, but return to the vision. Clarity will bring strategy, and strategy will bring stability.

Your "Why" Must Be Stronger Than the Wind

Without a strong *why*, every setback will feel like a reason to quit. But when your *why* is unshakable, you'll weather the storm instead of running from it. Entrepreneurs who succeed are not the ones who never face difficulties; they are the ones whose purpose is greater than their pain.

Consider the apostle Paul, who endured shipwrecks, beatings, and imprisonments yet never abandoned his mission. Why? Because his vision of spreading the gospel was bigger than his suffering. In the same way, your business must be anchored in a vision strong enough to keep you from quitting when the waves rise. Anchored entrepreneurs stand the test of time. Storms are temporary, but a business built on a firm vision is enduring. History proves that those who refuse to let go of their vision ultimately succeed. Think of Thomas Edison, who failed thousands of times before creating the lightbulb. His vision anchored him through failure. Think of Sarah Breedlove (Madam C.J. Walker), who faced racism, poverty, and rejection but became the first female "self-made" millionaire in America. Her vision of empowering Black women with haircare products anchored her through opposition.

The same will be true for you. You are building something greater than a business; you are building a legacy. And legacies are not built by those who abandon ship at the first sign of struggle. They are built by those who throw down the anchor, hold fast to their vision, and ride the storm with faith.

Storms will come, but your anchor is your vision. Don't abandon ship when the winds blow. Dig deeper into your *why*, listen for God's direction, and trust that He who called you will sustain you. Your business is bigger than just making money; it is a vessel for His kingdom. Stay on course, and watch God take you beyond what you could have imagined.

21

It's God's Business

One October morning, I found myself sitting on my back porch, just soaking in a rare moment of stillness. Janelle, my toddler, was napping inside, and I was about seven months pregnant with Josiah. Later that afternoon, I was scheduled to work a temp shift as a dental hygienist. But on that quiet morning, I had a window to breathe and reflect. I wanted to make the most of that sacred pause by reading my Bible.

At the time, I had just begun taking my social media journey seriously. I was preparing to release my *Eagle, Find Your Voice* prayer journal, and I knew that launching anything (especially as a Christian entrepreneur) required more than just showing up with a product. Anyone who's ever tried to sell something knows: You don't just post a flyer and expect a harvest. You need to show up consistently, serve your audience, and create value well before you ever make an offer. You need to *minister* before you *market*.

That morning, as I sat with my Bible, God gave me a clear and simple content idea; one that would help me show up in authenticity and truth. He said, "Share three Bible gems from what you read each day." That idea became my rhythm, and through it, God began to stir deeper purpose in my content and my calling.

That day, He led me to **Genesis 40**. I was reading the NLT version, and something leapt off the page like I'd never seen before.

In Genesis 40, Joseph is in prison, held alongside two men from Pharaoh's court: the baker and the butler. Both men had troubling dreams, and they couldn't understand what the dreams meant. Joseph responded to them with a peculiar but powerful statement:

"And they replied, 'We both had dreams last night, but no one can tell us what they mean.' 'Interpreting dreams is God's business,' Joseph replied. 'Go ahead and tell me your dreams.'" —**Genesis 40:8 (NLT)**

That phrase, **"Interpreting dreams is God's business"**, stopped me in my tracks.

Sure, interpreting dreams may not be what we think of when we say "business." But Joseph's mindset revealed something critical: he didn't take credit for his gift. He didn't pretend the ability to interpret dreams was something he mastered or marketed. He immediately gave **glory** to the Source—**God**.

And that moment illuminated a truth that I knew had to be written into the heart of every faith-driven entrepreneur:

Your gifts are God's business.

Whether you sing, sell, strategize, coach, write, teach, bake, build, or serve—**your ability is on loan from Heaven**. And every business you birth, every product you launch, every room you walk into; it's all God's business.

Business With the Right Foundation

When Joseph said, "Interpreting dreams is God's business," he didn't just make a passing statement. He was laying a foundation. And that foundation would carry him from obscurity to influence. From prison to the palace. From barely noticed to second-in-command in the most powerful nation of his time.

Joseph went on to interpret Pharaoh's dream with such divine precision that Pharaoh said:

"Can we find anyone else like this man so obviously filled with the spirit of God?" —**Genesis 41:38 (NLT)**

When you give glory to God in the small moments, He will trust you with visibility, favor, and increase. But you must be rooted in the truth that **the business doesn't belong to you; it belongs to God**.

The Shift That Changes Everything

You may be building a brand, launching a product, growing a following, but the deeper truth is: **you're stewarding God's assignment**. The moment you acknowledge that He is the CEO of your business and the Giver of every good gift, you invite Him to do what only He can do: elevate you beyond your ability.

"Work willingly at whatever you do, as though you were working for the Lord rather than for people" —**Colossians 3:23 (NLT)**

When you give Him the glory, He opens doors no man can shut. He places you in rooms you didn't have the credentials for. He positions you to bless others, not just with products or services, but with *purpose* and *presence*.

From the Pit to the Palace

Joseph's journey is not a fairytale. It was marked by betrayal, hardship, waiting, and obedience. But every stage (pit,

Potiphar's house, prison) was preparation for the palace. And none of it would have made sense without God at the center.

Your journey in business might feel like that too. You may be in the pit right now; overlooked, underfunded, or uncertain. Or you might feel like you're stuck in a prison of fear, comparison, or financial pressure. But when you keep giving God the glory, you give Him room to promote you.

Eventually, Joseph didn't just interpret dreams, he *lived* the dream. He became the strategic solution to a national crisis. He saved a nation. He restored his family. And it all started with one act of surrender: *"Interpreting dreams is God's business."*

Life More Abundantly

Joseph's promotion wasn't just about power; it was about purpose. God positioned him to preserve lives during a famine. Likewise, your business isn't just about making money. It's about making an impact. It's about *eternal life*—Zōē Aiōnios.

"I have come that they may have life, and have it to the full." **—John 10:10 (NIV)**

The Greek word **Zōē** refers to life that's vibrant, real, and active, life that overflows. God desires that you live a life of abundance in *every* way: spiritually, emotionally, mentally, and financially.

And here's the key: **that abundance starts with surrender.**

When you make it God's business, He makes it fruitful.

Reflection + Activation

- Where in your business have you taken the credit for what God gave you?

- What would it look like for you to consistently give God glory in your work, words, and wins?

- Are there ways God is asking you to surrender your plans so He can establish His?

- Are you building for visibility or for eternal impact?

22

Don't trust AI (Achan's Intelligence)

In the book of Joshua, we witness one of the most profound transitions in biblical history; the move from promise to possession. God had spoken clearly to Joshua and the children of Israel, reaffirming a covenant first established with Abraham. He promised them this: *"Every place that the sole of your foot will tread upon I have given to you, just as I promised to Moses"* (Joshua 1:3, ESV).

This was not a vague blessing. It was a divine guarantee. But while the promise was secure, the path to fulfillment required obedience. It required step-by-step instructions for every battle, every city, every possession. This is where many of us falter. We receive the promise but abandon the process. We want the inheritance but disregard the instruction.

Jericho was the first major conquest after Israel crossed the Jordan River into the Promised Land. It was a fortified city, impossible to penetrate by human standards.

But God had a strategy. Not a military strategy, but a divine one. He instructed them to walk in silence for six days around the city walls. Then on the seventh day, after circling seven times, the priests were to blow the trumpets, and the people were to shout. That shout would activate heaven's intervention, and the walls would fall.

Joshua relayed these instructions with precision:

"Shout! For the Lord has given you the city! The city and all that is in it are to be devoted to the Lord. Only Rahab the prostitute and all who are with her in her house shall be spared... But keep away from the devoted things, so that you will not bring about your own destruction by taking any of them." (Joshua 6:16-18, NLT)

God's instructions were specific:

1. **Rescue Rahab and her household** as a reward for her faith and protection of the spies.

2. **Dedicate all silver, gold, bronze, and iron to the Lord's treasury**—a first fruit offering from the land.

3. **Avoid the accursed or devoted things**—objects associated with idol worship, defilement, or destruction.

4. **Destroy the rest**—a cleansing act to honor

God's holiness.

This wasn't about controlling behavior. It was about preserving the covenant. God wanted their hearts, not just their actions.

Trusting Self Over God

There was a man apart from the Israelites named Achan. Achan violated the covenant by secretly taking a Babylonian garment, silver, and gold from Jericho. His decision cost Israel their next battle at Ai (The next land they were going to take.) Ai was a much smaller city in comparison to Jericho. It should have been an easy victory for the Israelites. Instead, 36 men died, fear spread through the camp, and God's presence was momentarily lifted.

When Joshua sought God in confusion, the Lord responded bluntly: get up! *"Israel has sinned; they have violated my covenant"* (Joshua 7:11). One man's disobedience affected an entire nation.

Achan had trusted in his own understanding. He saw riches and thought: *Why destroy what could benefit me?* But what he gained in the short term, he lost in the long term. Not only did he die, but so did his entire household. Meanwhile, when Israel obeyed God's strategy for the second battle at Ai, they not only won—they were allowed to plunder the entire city. The very thing Achan craved, God was ready to release—just not on Achan's terms.

A Modern Parallel: Building Businesses With God

Let's bring this home. Just like Achan's disobedience directly affected him, his family and entire nation, what decision can you make as a business owner that could impact others around you? Here's another question I want you to really think about. What is God asking you to leave behind that you've been secretly holding onto? Is there a "Babylonian garment" in your heart (something flashy, desirable, even lucrative) that God has already marked as off-limits? Is there any "silver or gold" that should have been given to Him that you kept for yourself? That can look like glory, attributes, and even money He told you to bless someone else with.

In the realm of entrepreneurship, especially for Christians navigating online business, the temptations are real. They can look like a business model that compromises your values, a partnership that seems profitable but lacks peace, or even a marketing strategy that gets attention but grieves your spirit.

Let's be clear: not every opportunity is a God-opportunity.

As entrepreneurs, we must move with spiritual intelligence, not just market intelligence. This doesn't mean we ignore tools like analytics, automation, and yes, even artificial intelligence (AI). But it does mean that we don't worship them. We don't idolize them. We don't trust them more than we trust the Holy Spirit.

Even in a digital age, the voice of God is still the most powerful strategy tool available. Artificial intelligence may offer leverage, but it can never replace authentic intelligence—the wisdom that comes from above. Business built on human brilliance alone will eventually crumble. Business built on God's voice will endure.

Lessons From the Fall and Rise of Israel

The story of Achan isn't just a warning. It's also a redemptive reminder that obedience restores access. After Achan was dealt with, Israel conquered Ai. They were re-connected with God's instruction and breakthroughs followed. Reflect on this:

- Are you trying to make something happen in your own strength?

- Are you holding on to people, patterns, or platforms that God said to release?

- Have you taken something prematurely that God intended to give you later?

Don't let impatience rob you of a generational reward. Don't let disobedience disqualify you from the very thing God desires to give you—abundantly.

You are not just a businesswoman or businessman. You are a builder in God's economy. That means your processes must be purified. Your victories must be rooted in righteousness. God is not just after your profits, He's after your partnership.

Let the story of Jericho and Ai anchor this truth in your spirit: **God's way is always better.** What He has for you is greater than anything you could gather for yourself. The reward of obedience will always outweigh the cost of compromise.

Trust Him in your business. Trust Him in your brand. Trust Him in your next launch, your next hire, your next pivot. Whether you're walking around a fortified wall or facing a small city like Ai, move only when He says move—and watch walls fall, resources multiply, and victory be assured.

SYSTEMIZE YOUR BUSINESS

23

Systems!

It was an ordinary summer afternoon in Chicago—a city buzzing with life, but not always with hope. A young boy made his way down the cracked sidewalk with a few crumpled dollars in his pocket. He was headed toward a simple joy: his favorite ice cream cone with rainbow sprinkles.

In a house full of siblings and raised by a single mother, treats like this probably felt like an escape. Life had been hard, but this small indulgence made it all feel bearable, if only for a moment.

As he approached the ice cream shop, his steps slowed. Parked across the street was something he had never seen up close before: a sleek Lamborghini. It wasn't just a car; it was a contradiction to everything he had grown up knowing about money, struggle, and limits.

Compelled by curiosity, he crossed the street and struck up a conversation with the driver—a young man, not much older than a college student. Their conversation lasted less than a minute, but that moment changed everything. In those twenty seconds, a new identity was born inside the boy. He wasn't just a kid from the South Side anymore. He was a future millionaire. A visionary. A builder.

That young boy was **MJ DeMarco**, and that day marked the beginning of his journey toward financial freedom. Years later, he would go on to build a multi-million dollar business empire rooted in one foundational truth: **wealth isn't built by trading time for money; it's built by creating systems**. In his book *The Millionaire Fastlane*, DeMarco shares that true financial freedom comes from scalable, automated systems that generate income without constant involvement. Not hustle. Not grinding endlessly. But systems: repeatable loops that turn action into outcomes on autopilot.

It's a philosophy that flies in the face of what many of us were taught. We're trained to work hard, climb ladders, and earn our way forward hour by hour. But DeMarco learned and proved that freedom comes not from doing more, but from building smarter. I'll be honest, I didn't fully grasp the power of systems until 2024. Up to that point, I had been praying fervently, asking God for favor, open doors, and divine acceleration. I had big dreams, undeniable vision, and the faith to match. But I was missing something crucial: **Structure.**

One day, during a quiet time of prayer, I cried out again: "Lord, where is the breakthrough? Where are the blessings You promised?" Starting a business, community or brand can be hard. I started feeling burnout. And just as clearly, I heard the Lord whisper back: **"Daughter, I've already given you favor. You just need systems to contain the favor and blessings that come with it."**

- That sentence hit me like a lightning bolt. It shifted my entire understanding of success. Favor (for business) without systems is like rain on cracked, dry ground—much of it is lost because there's nothing in place to catch, hold, or channel it. That's when it clicked: systems are the containers for sustained favor. They are the infrastructure that supports overflow. Without systems, even the blessings of God can leak through your hands.

- I love to imagine the Bible not just as a spiritual guide, but as a divine manual full of systems. These systems are God's brilliant, ordained frameworks that govern how life, family, and even business should operate.

- From Genesis to Revelation, God displays these

systems. He's strategic, intentional, and methodical. Think about it:

- Creation wasn't chaotic. It unfolded over six days in a clear sequence.

- The family structure wasn't accidental. There were roles, responsibilities, and generational blessing transfers.

- The tabernacle was built with precise blueprints and a rhythm of sacrifice, offering, and worship.

- The seasons, festivals, and laws were all set up on calendars and cycles.

- Jesus Himself didn't just preach. He discipled those who followed Him. He delegated to those He needed to. He **systemized** the Gospel so it could be carried to the ends of the earth through you and me.

When you start to see the Bible through this lens, you realize that many of the stories we grew up learning are not just spiritual illustrations; they are strategic systems that can be applied to modern life and business. In fact, if you're building a business as a believer, you're not starting from scratch. God has already laid out prototypes of success throughout His Word.

Let me show you a few of these biblical systems and how they directly connect to your business growth today:

CRM, or Customer Relationship Management:

CRM is a system used by businesses to manage interactions with current and potential customers. It involves utilizing technology to automate and synchronize sales, marketing, customer service, and technical support efforts. This is done to improve customer relationships in efforts to grow the business. CRM systems help track customer interactions, supporting sales processes and enhancing overall customer satisfaction.

While the Bible does not explicitly show men or women having a CRM system in place, many had helpers, handmaidens and servants. Gehazi for example was Elisha's servant who sometimes was the "first man" a person would see. He asked the Shunamite woman "Is it well with thee?" when she came back to see Elisha after her son died. He was the one who theologians believed initially spoke to Naaman when he came to Elisha for healing. He certainly was the one who went to Naaman after his healing and tried to get money. I'm not implying that Gehazi was the CRM for Elisha. However it's assuredly clear that having Gehazi in place eased Elisha's workload as a prophet of God tremendously.

HR, or Human Resources:

In the business world, Human Resources (HR) is the backbone of employee management; overseeing recruitment, onboarding, training, development, compliance, and even termination. HR ensures that every person functions within the company's values and vision. Similarly, in Daniel chapter 6, we see King Darius establishing an HR-like system over his vast empire. After dividing his kingdom into over 120 provinces and appointing high officers to manage each, he installs a higher tier of oversight: three administrators (one of whom was Daniel) to supervise the officers. This strategic move ensured accountability and protected the king's interests, much like how an HR department keeps an organization running smoothly by watching over those in authority.

Spiritually, the Holy Spirit serves as the divine HR in the Kingdom of God. While the apostles taught us the laws and values of the Kingdom, it is ultimately the Holy Spirit who manages our development. In the early stages when we are recruited into God's kingdom through salvation and baptism in Jesus' name, we must then have a true encounter with HR, which is the Holy Spirit. When He enters, He gives us a new language (heavenly), unique only to this kingdom. He trains us to reflect Christ, disciplines and corrects us when needed, and even has the authority to "terminate" our active use if we rebel. We never want to find ourselves in the position of operating in gifts but the anointing left us (as in 1 Samuel 16:14, when the Spirit departed from Saul). It is one of the most sobering realities: to think you're working for God when you've already been dismissed. Thankfully, when we remain aligned, the Holy Spirit--our access to the kingdom of God--also delivers our benefits: grace, fruit, and the powerful gifts outlined in 1 Corinthians 12:4–11 and Romans 12:6–8. He is not just our guide; He is our Kingdom HR—securing our calling, equipping us, and keeping us compliant with Heaven's standards.

Project Management System

Project management can often be seen as a modern concept. But when we look through the Bible with a business lens, we find a powerful, ancient example of project leadership in **Nehemiah**, who led the rebuilding of Jerusalem's wall. His approach mirrors what we now call a **project management system**, filled with vision casting, strategic planning, team delegation, crisis management, and timely execution.

Vision Fuels the Project

Every successful project starts with a compelling vision. Nehemiah was a cupbearer to the king in exile, but when he heard that Jerusalem's walls were in ruins, he was deeply moved.

"When I heard these things, I sat down and wept. For some days I mourned and fasted and prayed before the God of heaven." – **Nehemiah 1:4 (NIV)**

Nehemiah didn't leap into action without prayer and planning. He took his burden to God first. This is the first pillar of any God-centered business project: get aligned with God before making a move. Before launching a new business idea, offer, or digital product, pause and pray. Let the burden for your audience lead to a God-inspired vision. That vision becomes your project's **"why."**

Strategic Planning and Pitching Frames the Project

After prayer, Nehemiah approached King Artaxerxes with a strategic plan. He didn't just say, "Let me go rebuild." He presented a timeline, resource request, and purpose.

"If it pleases the king... send me to the city... so that I can rebuild it." – **Nehemiah 2:5**

"And because the gracious hand of my God was on me, the king granted my requests." – **Nehemiah 2:8**

Nehemiah is acting like a project manager pitching to a stakeholder. He's clear, confident, and solution-oriented. As entrepreneurs, we must be able to present our vision clearly, whether it's to a business partner, customer, investor, or team. God gives the vision, but it's up to us to articulate it with wisdom and clarity.

Organization and Delegation Fortifies the Project

Nehemiah didn't build the wall himself. He organized the work by family groups, gates, and sections. Each person had a role and location, and Nehemiah oversaw it all.

"Next to them, repairs were made by the men of Jericho, and next to them Zakkur son of Imri." – **Nehemiah 3:2**

This chapter reads like a *project management dashboard*. It has tasks assigned, progress tracked, and it even has all the teams grouped by zones. As business leaders, we must break big goals into small, manageable tasks. We should also assign them well, and follow up. No leader can or should do it alone. Nehemiah shows us the power of **systems and structure.**

Facing Opposition and Managing Crisis

Every project will meet resistance. In Nehemiah's case, enemies like **Sanballat and Tobiah** tried to distract and discourage the builders.

"They all plotted together to come and fight against Jerusalem and stir up trouble against it. But we prayed to our God and posted a guard day and night." – **Nehemiah 4:8-9**

Nehemiah's response? Prayer and action. He didn't ignore the threats, but he didn't let them derail the mission. He adjusted the plan. Business comes with spiritual warfare, criticism, and challenges. A wise leader doesn't panic. We pray, pivot, and protect the mission. Crisis management is part of good project management.

"From that day on, half of my men did the work, while the other half were equipped with spears..."

– **Nehemiah 4:16**

"So the wall was completed... in fifty-two days. When all our enemies heard about this, all the surrounding nations

were afraid... and realized that this work had been done with the help of our God." – **Nehemiah 6:15-16**

You may not be building a literal wall, but you're building **offers, platforms, courses, brands, and wealth systems** that require order, leadership, and diligence. Just like Nehemiah, you can complete what you start Just make God your CEO and you remain His faithful project manager.

"Commit to the Lord whatever you do, and he will establish your plans." – **Proverbs 16:3 (NIV)**

Sales Funnel System

A sales funnel is the step-by-step process a potential customer goes through from first discovering your brand to ultimately making a purchase and essentially joining your community. It's called a "funnel" because the masses enter at the top, but only a smaller number make it all the way through to the bottom. I'll show you the example of a "sales funnel" through the life of Jesus. Though Jesus wasn't trying to sell anything to anyone (salvation was free for all), He did show up consistently to a large mass of people. He became the most influential person of His time, attracting millions of people to Himself. While everyone listened, not everyone trickled down the funnel. Let's first look at a sales funnel, then see how Jesus can be seen in it.

The top of the funnel is "Awareness"

The first stage of a sales funnel is *awareness*—this is when a potential customer first discovers you. Whether it's through a viral Instagram reel, a blog post, a YouTube video, a paid ad, or a friend's referral, visibility is the starting point. In business, this is intentional marketing; in the Kingdom, we see Jesus master this principle. Though Jesus wasn't selling anything (salvation is free to all of us), He strategically placed Himself in high-traffic and highly visible environments. Places like seashores where fishermen and merchants worked, on mountains where crowds gathered for teaching, and in cities where the culture and conflict were alive. He didn't hide His message behind closed doors; He funneled people in through visibility. His "ads" were miracles. His "content" was parables. His "platform" was wherever people were. His copywriter abilities? Impeccable. He said things like "Before Abraham was, I AM" a phrase that almost got him killed but pulled even more people to His teachings. Just as a strong funnel begins with public exposure to draw interest, Jesus opened His funnel by showing up where people already were and offering a message that addressed both spiritual hunger and practical life. The principle remains the same today: you can't lead people to truth or transformation if they don't first know you exist.

The next part is "Interest"

The next stage in the funnel is *interest*—this is when someone moves beyond casual awareness and becomes curious about what you truly offer. Maybe they saw your content and something resonated. Now they click the link in your bio, explore your free resource, or scroll deeper into your page. Their curiosity becomes a small commitment. Jesus modeled this beautifully. While He didn't have a landing page or digital funnel, He knew how to filter the crowd and call out the curious. After speaking to the masses, He often shifted His focus to the few—those whose hearts stirred enough to take the next step. His invitation was simple but powerful: "Follow me." These two words weren't shouted to the crowd—they were extended to individuals who had seen or heard just enough to want more. Interest isn't about information; it's about attraction. And Jesus knew how to attract those who were spiritually hungry. In business and ministry alike, the interest stage is where the seed of transformation is planted. You're no longer just visible—you're becoming valuable.

The next part of the funnel is "Consideration"

The next stage is *consideration*—this is where the potential customer seriously evaluates whether your offer meets their needs or solves their problem. They're no longer just curious; they're thinking, comparing, and counting the cost. In business, this might look like someone watching your webinar, reading testimonials, or opening your email sequence multiple times. They're leaning in, but not yet all in. In the ministry of Jesus, this stage is reflected in those who followed Him beyond the crowd—like the 72 disciples. These were people who had moved past curiosity. They traveled with Him, listened intently, and even carried out assignments in His name. But when His message required deeper sacrifice—when He said things that challenged their comfort or called for radical obedience—many turned back. Luke 9 and John 6 show this moment clearly: people considered the cost and decided the commitment wasn't for them. In your funnel, not everyone who's interested will continue. Some will opt out when they realize what you offer requires change, discipline, or faith. That's okay. The *consideration* stage is where your clarity matters most—because those who do move forward are no longer casual observers. They're preparing to invest.

John 6:60 - *Therefore many of His disciples, when they heard this, said, "This is a hard saying; who can understand it?*

John 6:66-67 - *From that time many of His disciples went back and walked with Him no more. Then Jesus said to the twelve, "Do you also want to go away?"*

In John 6:60-71, Jesus says a "*hard saying*" that most of the disciples could not understand. That day, the majority of them walked away leaving only 12. They decided that walking with Jesus was not for them. And so, further down the funnel we go.

The bottom of the funnel leads to Conversion

The bottom of the funnel leads to *conversion*—this is the moment when a person takes decisive action. In business, this is when the potential customer becomes an actual customer: they purchase your course, book your service, or invest in your offer. It's the fulfillment of every step before it. For Jesus, though He wasn't selling products, He extended the greatest offer of all: salvation, purpose, and eternal life. His "conversion" moment wasn't transactional—it was transformational. In Mark 3:13–14, we see Jesus go up on a mountain and *call out the ones He wanted*. "And they came to Him," the passage says. This is conversion in its purest form. These twelve men were more than followers; they became apostles—those sent with power and purpose. They moved from listening in the crowd to living on mission. Jesus didn't just capture their attention; He captured their hearts. Just like in a sales funnel, conversion is never the end—it's the beginning of a new relationship. In Kingdom business, the goal is not just a sale, but a soul aligned with God's call. And when conversion is real, commitment follows.

Loyalty & Advocacy (Beyond the Funnel)

The last and most powerful stage of the funnel—*loyalty and advocacy*—technically happens beyond the funnel itself. This is where transformation becomes multiplication. It's when customers are so deeply impacted by your offer that they return, stay connected, and begin to refer others. They become your brand ambassadors, not because they were paid, but because they were changed. In the Kingdom, Jesus modeled this through what I call "the faithful few." Among His twelve disciples, three stood out as uniquely loyal—Peter, James, and John. These weren't just followers; they were friends. They experienced Jesus in ways the others did not. They saw His glory at the Mount of Transfiguration, were invited to witness Jairus' daughter being raised from the dead, and were trusted in moments of both power and pain. In Mark 5, when doubt filled Jairus' house and everyone laughed at Jesus, He cleared the room—even removing nine of His own disciples. But Peter, James, and John remained. Why? Because their faith, loyalty, and intimacy had earned them access. These three didn't just consume what Jesus offered; they carried it. They later became bold advocates—writing books, preaching truth, and performing miracles that sparked the early church. Peter, despite once denying Jesus, became a cornerstone in the Jewish-to-Christian movement. That's what real advocacy looks like. It's born from encounter and sustained by devotion. In your business or ministry, your most loyal followers won't just buy—they'll build with you, speak for you, and expand your impact far beyond what you could do alone.

Maintenance of systems

The biggest problem with systems that eventually break down is not that they were faulty from the start—it's that they were neglected. Systems, no matter how well-designed, require maintenance. James Clear, in his book *Atomic Habits*, points out a hidden danger in the power of automation: once a habit becomes automatic, it stops demanding your attention. While automation can free up mental space and streamline your life, it can also make you blind to the slow breakdowns happening beneath the surface.

Just like a thriving plant follows a natural, systematic process—growing roots, sprouting stems, producing fruit—its health depends on ongoing care. If the soil is depleted, if weeds grow unchecked, or if pruning is neglected, that same plant can become overgrown, unfruitful, or even die. Systems need watchfulness, and so do we.

We see this illustrated powerfully in Daniel chapter 4. King Nebuchadnezzar had a dream of a massive, flourishing tree that reached to the heavens. It was beautiful, abundant, and provided shelter for many. But in his pride, he forgot the Source of his greatness. He neglected the spiritual system that upheld him. In verse 13, a holy watcher from heaven came with a decree: the tree was to be cut down, leaving only the stump and its roots. That stump represented mercy—a remnant, a chance to rebuild—but the lofty system that had once stood tall was brought low because of unchecked pride.

This story is a sobering metaphor for entrepreneurs and leaders. Your first system—before the marketing funnels, product pipelines, or content strategies—is the system of your heart. The condition of your inner life governs everything else. If your heart is unguarded, if pride sneaks in, or if you start running on autopilot without acknowledging God, your systems will suffer. Leadership without humility leads to collapse.

So, maintain your heart like you would a vital system. Seek God daily. Invite Him into your decisions. Remember, it's the Almighty who gave you your gifts, your platform, and your influence. Don't become the tree that grew tall only to be chopped down.

And let this principle guide how you manage your business systems too. Schedule regular time to review what's working and what's weakening. Is your customer journey smooth? Are your processes scalable? Are your team dynamics healthy? If there's a breach, patch it. If there's inefficiency, prune it. Systems thrive under stewardship. Growth without maintenance leads to collapse. But growth with humility and care creates longevity.

24

Conclusion

This chapter ends the book, but starts with your new journey in entrepreneurship. My hope is that it uncovers powerful, often overlooked business principles embedded within the pages of the Bible; principles that have stood the test of time, economies, and empires.

Throughout these pages, we have examined stories and scriptures that reveal how God's people built, stewarded, and scaled wealth. From Abraham's faith-filled ventures to Ruth's strategic alignment, from Nehemiah's leadership blueprint to Proverbs' wisdom on diligence and planning, the Bible offers a rich tapestry of entrepreneurial insight.

This book equips you to:

- **Start** your business by aligning with God's vision, hearing His voice, and identifying your God-given gifts and marketplace calling.

- **Scale** your business by applying biblical strategies

like proper stewardship, principles of sowing and reaping, honoring partnerships, and building the right team.

- **Systemize** your business through divine order, structure, and wisdom found in stories like Moses leading Israel, Joseph organizing Egypt, and Jesus multiplying resources.

Every principle shared is anchored in Scripture and paired with modern-day business relevance. These lessons are not theoretical; they are transformational. Whether you are a new entrepreneur or a seasoned builder, the Bible holds a blueprint for supernatural success, wealth creation, and legacy-building.

As you reflect on what you've read, remember this: God is not absent from the marketplace. He is the Master Strategist, the Ultimate CEO, and the source of all creativity and increase. When you do business with Him and through Him, you will unlock not only financial fruitfulness but eternal fulfillment. I've seen it time and time again in my personal life.

This is more than business—this is Kingdom advancement. So let me take this opportunity to invite you to Christ, if you don't know Him already. He is more than a saver of your business, He is the Savior of the world! He died for our sins, and gave us hope to walk in the newness of life. If you already know Him and have accepted Him, keep walking with Him. The journey gets rough, but He will never leave you. From my heart to yours, may your business grow in abundance. May you continue to gain insight beyond this book, from the Bible, with your business lens.

25

About the Author

De'Shanti Genus is a dynamic author, speaker, dental hygienist, and entrepreneur. She is the visionary and co-founder— with her husband, Tenoy Genus— of *The Purposed Eagle;* a faith-driven empowerment network. The Purposed Eagle hosts live worship based entrepreneurship events yearly. With a deep passion for God's Word and a commitment to helping others discover their divine purpose, De'Shanti has become a trusted voice in self development, business mentorship, and kingdom living.

De'Shanti and Tenoy are also the founders of Vizal, a business and book consultation company whose mission statement is "Vision Made Vital." From their signature 12-week coaching program *Build the Vision*, to masterclasses on passive income and business acceleration, she equips individuals with the tools and strategies to launch, and grow their businesses, and publish their best-selling books!

As a wife, mom, and entrepreneur, De'Shanti uniquely understands the intersection of faith, family, and entrepreneurship. She is the author of several transformational books, including *From Faith to Favor*, *Eagle, Find Your Voice*, *Eagle, Spread Your Wings*, and *Bible In Business Lens* which blend biblical truth with practical encouragement for those on a journey of spiritual growth and breakthrough. De'Shanti uses live video platforms, workshops, and digital products to reach a global audience ready to walk boldly in their calling.

She attends— and serves happily— at the Bethel Shiloh Apostolic Church, with her family, in Connecticut.

Connect with De'Shanti on social media platforms, and explore more resources at www.thepurposedeagle.com

NOTES

This section of the book includes all the notes and citations for each chapter. I understand that over the course of time, research advances. Sources are subject to change (aside from scriptural references). If any of these online links no longer exist by the time you read, allow me to make a preemptive apology. I hope you find this section helpful.

Chapter 1

1. **Biblical parallels**, particularly in 2 Kings 6–7, show that God's supernatural supply often comes in impossible circumstances. The famine in Samaria turned into abundance overnight, showing that timing is not a limitation for God.

2. **Doubt can disqualify** us from experiencing the blessings of God's economy, as shown by the offi-

cer in 2 Kings 7 who saw the provision but never partook in it.

3. **God still uses destiny helpers**—people strategically positioned to help fulfill your purpose, like the mortgage broker in this story who opened doors that money or status could not.

4. This chapter emphasizes that **faith in action, not just belief, is the currency of Heaven**. We must move when God says move, wait when He says wait, and trust Him even when things don't make sense.

Chapter 2

Key Scriptures Referenced

1. **Psalm 101:2–3 (NLT)**
   "I will be careful to live a blameless life... I will lead a life of integrity in my own home... I will refuse to look at anything vile and vulgar..."
   – These verses form the foundation of the chapter, showing the personal accountability and

heart posture of a righteous leader. David's commitment to walk in integrity becomes a blueprint for evaluating ourselves and the people we bring into our spheres of influence.

2. **Psalm 101:4–5 (NLT)**

"I will reject perverse ideas and stay away from every evil. I will not tolerate people who slander... or are proud."

– These verses highlight the types of people that can be detrimental to a healthy team. Integrity is not just personal—it's cultural. As a leader, it's vital to protect the environment of your organization.

3. **Psalm 101:6 (NLT)**

"I will search for faithful people to be my companions..."

– The mark of a true team member isn't just talent, it's faithfulness. David prioritized dependability and righteousness in his inner circle—this mirrors the kind of discernment modern Christian entrepreneurs should have.

4. **2 Samuel 16:23 (NLT)**

"Absalom followed Ahithophel's advice just as

David had done, for every word Ahithophel spoke seemed as wise as though it had come directly from the mouth of God."

– Though Ahithophel had immense wisdom, his betrayal of David proves that *skill without loyalty is dangerous*. This story emphasizes that a person's heart must be considered above their résumé.

Modern Business Reference

Richard Branson, the British billionaire and founder of **Virgin Group**, has often attributed his success to building and sustaining strong teams. In an interview covered by **CNBC** (Ruth Umoh, October 18, 2017)

  Citation:

Umoh, Ruth. *Richard Branson on what he looks for in employees*. CNBC, October 18, 2017. https://www.cnbc.com/2017/10/18/richard-branson-on-what-he-looks-for-in-employees.html

Takeaway Principles

1. **Leadership starts with self-examination**: Like David, evaluate your own heart and motives be-

fore inviting others into your vision.

2. **Culture is built by who you tolerate**: Eliminate gossip, pride, and hidden agendas early.

3. **Skill is secondary to heart posture**: Someone may have wisdom like Ahithophel but still carry the potential to sabotage.

4. **Faithfulness is the foundation of team-building**: Consistent, humble, and loyal people are rare—and priceless.

5. **Even secular success stories point to biblical wisdom**: Branson's emphasis on treating people well aligns with the heart of servant leadership in Scripture.

Chapter 3

Key Scriptures and Spiritual Themes

1. **Genesis 6:13–22 (NLT)**
   "So Noah did everything exactly as God had commanded him."

– Noah's obedience, even when God's instructions seemed radical and unreasonable, is a powerful example of **faith-fueled building**. Noah followed divine instruction without needing public validation. For modern entrepreneurs, this means staying committed to God's vision even when others don't understand.

2. **Genesis 7:1–5 (NLT)**

"Enter the boat with all your family… Do everything as I have commanded."

– Not only was Noah obedient, but he also moved in **God's timing**, which is essential in both spiritual and business ventures. Delayed or premature movement outside of divine instruction can lead to unnecessary hardship.

3. **Hebrews 11:7 (NLT)**

"It was by faith that Noah built a large boat to save his family from the flood. He obeyed God… and he received the righteousness that comes by faith."

– This verse situates Noah among the faith giants. His willingness to build without physical evidence of rain parallels our call to **build businesses, ministries, and movements in faith**, trusting that God will fulfill what He promised.

4. **Matthew 11:28–30 (NLT)**

"Come to me, all of you who are weary and carry heavy burdens, and I will give you rest... For my yoke is easy to bear, and the burden I give you is light."

– This New Testament verse affirms the paradox of **movement with rest**. God's yoke doesn't mean no work—it means the work is graced. You can be in motion without striving or burnout when you're aligned with God's plan.

Key Concepts for Entrepreneurs and Builders

1. **Rest is not the absence of activity—it's the presence of God.**

   The paradox of *"move with rest"* becomes clear when you realize rest in God doesn't mean inactivity, but working from a place of peace, alignment, and confidence in divine timing.

2. **Delayed gratification leads to sustained success.**

   Just like Noah, building something worthwhile often requires sacrificing short-term pleasures for long-term purpose. This applies to finances, time, energy, and relationships.

3. **Obedience is the currency of movement.**
   In your business and life, **faithful obedience** is what moves the hand of God. Noah didn't build with logic—he built with trust.

4. **Provision follows obedience.**
   The testimony about building The Purposed Eagle Network reflects this principle. When the work feels overwhelming, God responds to surrendered prayer and sends help—sometimes supernaturally.

5. **God sends the right people when you move in purpose.**
   Just like Noah built with his family and you built with your core team, divine alignment brings the right community. God never intends for us to build alone.

Modern Definitions and Observations

1. **Noah = "Rest"** (Hebrew origin)
   This definition turns the phrase *"Move with Noah"* into a prophetic revelation: *"Move with*

rest." It's a call to action without anxiety.

2. **Traverse** = "to pass or move over, along, or through; to journey across or through."
   This word emphasizes the forward momentum required in a faith walk, even when the road is uncharted.

Prophetic Insight

1. **Moving into a new Jewish year (5784 → 5785)**
   Jewish new years represent spiritual crossover points—times of divine reset and forward progression. Your story of hearing from God at this juncture echoes biblical patterns of transition, such as when Noah stepped into a new world after the flood (Genesis 8).

2. **The Builder's Anointing**
   This chapter speaks prophetically to entrepreneurs, visionaries, and creators who are being called to build God-aligned projects in this season. The reminder? Don't just build—*build with God.* That's the safest, most fruitful place to be.

Chapter 4

Key Scriptures and Biblical Examples

1. "Ehud reached with his left hand, pulled out the dagger strapped to his right thigh, and plunged it into the king's belly... Then Ehud closed and locked the doors of the room and escaped." (v. 21–23)**Judges 3:12–26 (NLT)** – *The Story of Eglon and Ehud*

    - Though Eglon was an oppressive ruler, this passage uniquely illustrates how **Ehud had to get close**—to position himself strategically—before he could deliver Israel. Symbolically, only for the purposes of this book, the "fat" (Eglon's description) represents stored-up resources, insight, or influence. This is a picture of how God can use proximity for positioning—even when the source doesn't look godly.

2. "Wisdom is the principal thing; therefore get wisdom: and with all thy getting get understanding." **Proverbs 4:7 (KJV)**

- This verse serves as your chapter's anchor. Wisdom can come in unconventional packages, but discernment helps determine how to apply it. **Knowledge + Understanding = Strategic Growth.**

3. "God gave these four young men an unusual aptitude for understanding every aspect of literature and wisdom..." **Daniel 1:3–4, 17 (NLT)** – *Daniel and the Hebrew boys in Babylon*

    - Even though they were immersed in a pagan system, God gave them the ability to learn without compromising their faith. This shows that **learning from secular sources doesn't mean agreement** with ungodly values. It means using discernment to extract what is useful for God's purpose.

4. "Moses was taught all the wisdom of the Egyptians, and he was powerful in both speech and action." (Acts 7:22)**Exodus 2:10 / Acts 7:22 (NLT)** – *Moses in Pharaoh's palace*

    - Raised and educated in a pagan environment, **Moses' training later prepared him** for leadership, administration, and delivering God's people. His background was not a mistake—it was part of God's preparation.

5. "Since God has revealed the meaning of the dreams to you... you will be in charge of my court." **Genesis 41:39–40 (NLT)** – *Joseph and Pharaoh*

    ◦ Joseph was placed in high government leadership under Pharaoh and had to understand and manage Egyptian economics. He functioned within a worldly system with heavenly wisdom. This reinforces the idea that **God can elevate His people inside secular systems for divine impact.**

Key Principles and Takeaways

1. **Success leaves clues.**
   As quoted early on, learning from those who've done what you aspire to do is a proven growth principle. Their methods may not always look like yours, but their experience is a treasure chest when viewed through discernment.

2. **Proximity brings access.**
Just like Ehud had to get close to Eglon, sometimes God will position you near people you didn't expect in order to access wisdom or opportunity. Stay alert and humble enough to learn.

3. **Discernment is non-negotiable.**
As clarified: this is not about seeking wisdom from dark or ungodly sources (witches, mystics, or those dabbling in the occult). It's about learning **industry truths, business principles, and leadership lessons** from those who've walked ahead—*while remaining rooted in the Word.*

Modern Insights and Practical Wisdom

1. **Jim Rohn** — "Your level of success will rarely exceed your level of personal development." **"The greatest asset to your company is YOU."**
This timeless truth underscores the necessity of **personal development**, spiritual maturity, and internal growth in entrepreneurship. When you grow, your business grows.

2. **Mentorship doesn't always look like min-

istry.

Some of your greatest business breakthroughs may come from professionals, coaches, or retired entrepreneurs whose life experience carries weight—even if their theology doesn't align with yours.

Chapter 5

1. **Philippians 1:6 (NLT)** – *"And I am certain that God, who began the good work within you, will continue his work until it is finally finished on the day when Christ Jesus returns."*

    ◦ A reminder that God is the author and finisher of your assignment. This Scripture grounds the reader in the assurance that what God starts, He sustains and completes.

2. **Nehemiah 4:4–5 (NLT)** – Nehemiah's raw and honest prayer in the midst of attack shows us how to process opposition through prayer. Rather than retaliating in the flesh, Nehemiah responded by petitioning God directly.

    ◦ *"Then I prayed, 'Hear us, our God, for we are*

being mocked. May their scoffing fall back on their own heads..."

3. **Nehemiah 4:14 (NLT)** – Nehemiah points the people back to vision and legacy: *"Don't be afraid of the enemy! Remember the Lord, who is great and glorious, and fight for your brothers, your sons, your daughters, your wives, and your homes!"*

   ◦ A pivotal verse that emphasizes *why* we build—not just for ourselves, but for generations.

4. **Nehemiah 4:17 (NLT)** – *"The laborers carried on their work with one hand supporting their load and one hand holding a weapon."*

   ◦ A powerful image of dual focus—working and warring simultaneously. A critical principle for spiritual entrepreneurs.

5. **Nehemiah 6:3 (NLT)** – *"So I replied by sending this message to them: 'I am doing a great work, and I cannot come down. Why should I stop working to come and meet with you?'"*

   ◦ This verse encapsulates focus, discernment,

and purpose. A declaration for anyone who feels pulled away from their God-given assignment.

6. **Napoleon Hill, *Think and Grow Rich*** – The quote "Set your mind on a definite goal and observe how quickly the world stands aside to let you pass" reflects the universal principle of intense focus. Though Hill wrote from a secular success philosophy, this idea aligns with biblical calls to fix our eyes on the goal (Philippians 3:13–14).

7. **Matthew 19:26 (NLT)** – *"Jesus looked at them intently and said, 'Humanly speaking, it is impossible. But with God everything is possible.'"*

   ○ An anchor verse to inspire perseverance and faith when natural strength runs out. God's power makes the impossible attainable.

Chapter 6

1 Kings 3:5 (NLT) – *"That night the Lord appeared to Solomon in a dream, and God said, 'What do you want? Ask, and I will give it to you!'"*

- This divine invitation from God set the stage for

Solomon's entire reign. It's a powerful reminder that God's favor often comes with a question that demands wisdom in response.

1 Kings 3:9 (NLT) – *"Give me an understanding heart so that I can govern your people well and know the difference between right and wrong. For who by himself is able to govern this great people of yours?"*

- Solomon's humble yet strategic request for wisdom shows his deep understanding of leadership, stewardship, and the gravity of influence. His ask positioned him for legacy.

1 Kings 3:10–13 (NLT) –
"The Lord was pleased that Solomon had asked for wisdom. So God replied, 'Because you have asked for wisdom in governing my people with justice... I will give you what you asked for! I will give you a wise and understanding heart... And I will also give you what you did not ask for—riches and fame!'"

- This shows how asking for the *right* thing in God's economy often releases overflow. Solomon's story models how purpose can unlock profit.

James 1:5 (NLT) – *"If you need wisdom, ask our generous God, and he will give it to you. He will not rebuke you for asking."*

- This New Testament reinforcement confirms that the offer God made to Solomon is still extended to believers today. We have access to divine strategy—if we ask.

2 Chronicles 3:1 (NLT) – *"Then Solomon began to build the Temple of the Lord in Jerusalem on Mount Moriah, where the Lord had appeared to David, his father. This was the place that the Lord had chosen... to be the site of the Temple."*

- Solomon didn't just inherit a throne; he activated a vision. He took the blueprints his father couldn't build and executed them with excellence. A powerful metaphor for spiritual entrepreneurship.

Chapter 7

Ruth 1:16 (NLT) – *"But Ruth replied, 'Don't ask me to leave you and turn back. Wherever you go, I will go; wherever you live, I will live. Your people will be my people, and your God will be my God.'"*

- Ruth's bold decision to leave her homeland and follow Naomi was not just relational loyalty—it was spiritual alignment. This marked her first major investment: her *future*.

Ruth 2:2–3 (NLT) - *"One day Ruth the Moabite said to Naomi, 'Let me go out into the harvest fields to pick up the stalks of grain left behind by anyone who is kind enough to let me do it.' Naomi replied, 'All right, my daughter, go ahead.' So Ruth went out to gather grain behind the harvesters. And as it happened, she found herself working in a field that belonged to Boaz..."*

- This passage shows Ruth's willingness to take initiative with what little she had—her time and strength. Her labor became her investment.

Ruth 2:10–12 (NLT) - *"Boaz replied, 'I also know about everything you have done for your mother-in-law since the death of your husband... May the Lord, the God of Israel, under whose wings you have come to take refuge, reward you fully for what you have done.'"*

- Boaz acknowledges Ruth's character and sacrifice. Her faithfulness didn't go unnoticed—by man *or* by God.

Ruth 2:15–16 (NLT) – *"Boaz ordered his young men, 'Let her gather grain right among the sheaves without stopping her. And pull out some heads of barley from the bundles and drop them on purpose for her. Let her pick them up, and don't give her a hard time!'"*

- This is a picture of *intentional favor*. Ruth's diligence positioned her for blessings that exceeded her efforts.

Ruth 4:13–17 (NLT) – *"So Boaz took Ruth into his home, and she became his wife... They named him Obed. He became the father of Jesse and the grandfather of David."*

- Ruth's journey from outsider to ancestor of royalty reminds us that divine destiny often flows through everyday obedience. Her fieldwork became a generational pivot.

Matthew 1:5–6 (NLT) – *"Salmon was the father of Boaz (whose mother was Rahab). Boaz was the father of Obed (whose mother was Ruth). Obed was the father of Jesse. Jesse was the father of King David."*

- Ruth's inclusion in the genealogy of Christ is a testament to God's redemptive grace and her faithful investment. Her legacy outlived her labor.

Chapter 8

1. **Ruth 2:2–3 (NLT)** – *"One day Ruth the Moabite said to Naomi, 'Let me go out into the harvest fields to pick up the stalks of grain left behind by anyone who is kind enough to let me do it.' So Ruth went out to gather grain behind the harvesters..."*

   - Ruth's willingness to glean—without ownership or guarantee—models the principle of humble positioning. Her diligence in someone else's field laid the foundation for her divine elevation.

2. **Ruth 2:7 (NLT)** – *"She asked me this morning if she could gather grain behind the harvesters. She has been hard at work ever since..."*

   - Ruth's reputation of consistent labor and quiet faithfulness is what drew Boaz's attention. Her story proves that *presence and posture* can unlock opportunity.

3. **Proverbs 4:7 (NLT)** – *"Getting wisdom is the wisest thing you can do! And whatever else you do, develop good judgment."*

- Asking for wisdom is not just noble—it's necessary. Your willingness to seek and apply wisdom determines how far and how fast you'll grow.

Chapter 9

1. **Ecclesiastes 11:3 (KJV)**

   "If the clouds be full of rain, they empty themselves upon the earth..."

   → This Scripture sets the tone for the law of process and accumulation. It illustrates how consistent, gradual buildup eventually leads to visible manifestation. Rain doesn't fall at the first drop, but once the cloud is full—a metaphor for preparation meeting opportunity.

2. **Scientific Principle of Rain Formation**

   → Rain forms through condensation: water vapor collects in clouds, and when the cloud reaches saturation, gravity causes precipitation. This natural process aligns with the biblical metaphor, reinforcing the value of slow, steady buildup before overflow.

   Source: National Weather Service, weather.gov

3. **The Penny Doubling Riddle**

→ This thought experiment is often used to teach compound interest and exponential growth. A penny doubled every day for 30 days equals over **$5 million**, not just $1 million.

Example Calculation:

Day 1: $0.01

Day 2: $0.02

Day 30: $5,368,709.12

→ Principle: Consistent investment leads to exponential returns.

Source: "The Power of Compounding," *Investopedia*.

4. **Ecclesiastes 11:1–2 (NLT)**

"Send your grain across the seas, and in time, profits will flow back to you. But divide your investments among many places, for you do not know what risks might lie ahead."

→ Solomon's advice is deeply entrepreneurial: sow, diversify, and wait for return. It echoes modern investment strategies like diversification and delayed return.

Citation: Holy Bible, New Living Translation (NLT). Tyndale House Foundation.

5. **Nehemiah's Wall – Nehemiah 4:6 (NLT)**

   "At last the wall was completed to half its height around the entire city, for the people had worked with enthusiasm."

   → Nehemiah's team built the wall one section at a time. It's a biblical picture of diligent, focused work over time—brick by brick.

   Reference: Nehemiah 4; context: rebuilding Jerusalem's wall amidst opposition.

6. **Delayed vs. Instant Gratification**

   → The concept of delayed gratification is supported by psychological studies such as the "Stanford Marshmallow Experiment," which showed that children who delayed gratification often had better life outcomes.

   Source: Mischel, Walter. *The Marshmallow Test: Mastering Self-Control*. Little, Brown, 2014.

7. **Currency and Cash Flow Metaphor**

   → The use of water as a metaphor for money aligns with the idea of "currency" (from Latin *currere*, meaning "to flow"). Money is designed to move—invest, circulate, and grow—not stagnate.

   Commentary: This imagery encourages active

stewardship of finances and continual sowing.

8. **Biblical Wisdom Literature and Investment Themes**

→ Much of Ecclesiastes and Proverbs deal with wise stewardship, diligence, patience, and reward. These are spiritual and practical tools for business and life success.

Example: Proverbs 13:11 (NLT): *"Wealth from get-rich-quick schemes quickly disappears; wealth from hard work grows over time."*

Chapter 10

1. **Exodus 4:2 (NLT)** –

   "Then the Lord asked him, 'What is that in your hand?' 'A shepherd's staff,' Moses replied."

   – God redirects Moses from what he lacks to what he already has—illustrating how purpose often begins with what's already in reach.

2. **Exodus 7:10 (NLT)** –

   "So Moses and Aaron went to Pharaoh and did what the Lord had commanded them. Aaron threw down his staff before Pharaoh and his offi-

cials, and it became a serpent!"

– The same rod is used to demonstrate God's power to Pharaoh, marking the beginning of Moses' public ministry.

3. **Exodus 14:16 (NLT) –**

   "Pick up your staff and raise your hand over the sea. Divide the water so the Israelites can walk through the middle of the sea on dry ground."

   – A pivotal moment where the staff becomes the instrument through which the Red Sea is parted.

4. **Exodus 17:11 (NLT) –**

   "As long as Moses held up the staff in his hand, the Israelites had the advantage. But whenever he dropped his hand, the Amalekites gained the advantage."

   – This shows the spiritual authority and covering that came through Moses' obedience with what was in his hand.

5. **Zechariah 4:10 (NLT) –**

   "Do not despise these small beginnings, for the Lord rejoices to see the work begin..."

   – A direct affirmation of God's delight in humble starts and early obedience—reminding read-ers that starting small is not a flaw but a Kingdom principle.

Chapter 11

Strong's Concordance, "Pragmateuomai," *Blue Letter Bible*, accessed [may, 2025], https://www.blueletterbible.org/lexicon/g4231/kjv/tr/0-1/.

Strong's Concordance, "Yarash," *Bible Hub* https://biblehub.com/hebrews/3423.htm

"Hebrew Calendar," *Bible Hub*, accessed [2025],https://biblehub.com/calendar/.

Chapter 13

1. **Cultural Context of the Canaanite Woman** — As a Gentile, she was outside the covenant promises of Israel, yet her faith granted her access to divine intervention. This reflects the inclusive nature of the Kingdom of God, where spiritual hunger often overrides social barriers.

☐ See theological commentary on Matthew 15 in *The Expositor's Bible Commentary* or *NIV Application Commentary*.

2. **Business Analogy: "Crumbs" as Entry-Level Resources** — This metaphor relates free content (such as webinars, podcasts, and blog posts) to crumbs from the Master's table. In business, these often serve as accessible, valuable stepping stones for early-stage entrepreneurs.

☐ Godin, Seth. *The Dip: A Little Book That Teaches You When to Quit (and When to Stick)*. Portfolio, 2007.

☐ Stanford Graduate School of Business. "Free Resources for Aspiring Entrepreneurs." gsb.stanford.edu.

3. **Crumbs Are for Starting, Not Staying** — The chapter emphasizes that free resources are important for momentum but not sustainable for long-term growth. Wise investment in mentorship, education, and systems is essential for scale.

☐ Maxwell, John C. *Sometimes You Win, Sometimes You Learn*. Center Street, 2013.

☐ Proverbs 24:3–4 (NLT): "A house is built by wisdom and becomes strong through good sense.

Through knowledge its rooms are filled with all sorts of precious riches and valuables."

4. **Business Strategy Concept: A/B Testing** — This is a data-driven marketing practice where two versions of a piece of content are tested to see which performs better. It allows for iterative growth and clarity in messaging.
   ☐ Neil Patel. "What is A/B Testing?" neilpatel.com/what-is-ab-testing/
   ☐ Harvard Business Review. "The Right Way to AB Test Your Product." hbr.org.

5. **Spiritual Application for Entrepreneurs** — The faith of the Canaanite woman parallels the entrepreneurial journey—beginning in obscurity, fueled by hunger, and tested by process. Her persistence is a model for how faith-filled action opens doors, even with limited resources.

Chapter 14

1. **The Principle of Leverage in Business** — Leverage refers to using tools, systems, people, or strategies to multiply effort and reduce manu-

al input. This business principle aligns with the concept of operational scalability.

☐ Cialdini, Robert B. *Influence: The Psychology of Persuasion*. Harper Business, 2006.

☐ Gerber, Michael E. *The E-Myth Revisited: Why Most Small Businesses Don't Work and What to Do About It*. Harper Business, 1995.

2. **Transportation Analogy (Bike vs. Walking; Plane vs. Driving)** — Used here as a metaphor to demonstrate how leveraging tools (transportation, in this case) increases speed and efficiency in reaching goals.

☐ Sinek, Simon. *Start with Why: How Great Leaders Inspire Everyone to Take Action*. Portfolio, 2009.

3. **Michael Phelps as a Case Study in Natural Leverage** — Phelps' unique physical build serves as a real-world example of leveraging one's natural design to gain competitive advantage.

☐ Longman, Jeré. "Olympian Michael Phelps's Physique Is Suited to Swimming." *The New York Times*, 8 Aug. 2008. www.nytimes.com

4. **Scriptural Examples of Divine Leverage**:

- David and Goliath – 1 Samuel 17 (NLT).
- Moses and the Red Sea – Exodus 14:16 (NLT).
- Jesus feeding the multitude – Matthew 14:13–21 (NLT).
- BibleHub. "1 Samuel 17," "Exodus 14:16," and "Matthew 14:13–21." https://biblehub.com

5. **Catalyst as a Spiritual and Scientific Concept** — A catalyst increases the rate of a reaction without being consumed, used here metaphorically to describe the favor of God and divine intervention.

    - Holme, Thomas, et al. *Chemistry in Context*. 9th ed., McGraw-Hill Education, 2017.
    - Luke 2:52 (NIV): "And Jesus grew in wisdom and stature, and in favor with God and man."
    - BibleGateway. "Luke 2:52 (NIV)." https://www.biblegateway.com

Chapter 15

1. **Hagar and the Hidden Well** — In Genesis 21:14–19, Hagar, in a moment of desperation, is shown a well by God after crying out in distress. This illustrates that divine provision may already

be present—we simply need spiritual vision to recognize it.

☐ *The Holy Bible*. New Living Translation, Tyndale House Publishers, 2015. Genesis 21:14–19.

☐ BibleHub. "Genesis 21:14–19." https://biblehub.com

2. **The Samaritan Woman at the Well (John 4)** — Jesus' encounter with the woman of Samaria is a powerful example of divine interruption, personal restoration, and spiritual redefinition.

☐ *The Holy Bible*. New International Version, Zondervan, 2011. John 4:1–26.

☐ BibleGateway. "John 4 (NIV)." https://www.biblegateway.com

3. **Business and Depletion** — The metaphor of "dried-up bottles" refers to failed strategies, burnout, or unproductive outcomes in entrepreneurship. Entrepreneurs often operate from a place of depletion unless they're anchored by a deeper source.

☐ Hyatt, Michael. *Your Best Year Ever: A 5-Step Plan for Achieving Your Most Important Goals*. Baker Books, 2018.

☐ Pressfield, Steven. *The War of Art: Break*

Through the Blocks and Win Your Inner Creative Battles. Black Irish Entertainment, 2002.

Chapter 16

1. **John 5:2–9 (KJV)** — This passage recounts Jesus healing a man who had been lying at the pool of Bethesda for 38 years. The man represents many who wait passively for change instead of stepping into transformation.

   ☐ *The Holy Bible*. King James Version, Thomas Nelson, 1987. John 5:2–9.

   ☐ BibleHub. "John 5:2–9." https://biblehub.com

2. **Greek Word Study – "Impotent" (Akratēs)** — The Greek word used for "impotent" carries meanings such as powerless, weak, poor, and needy. It suggests not only physical limitation but also psychological and spiritual depletion.

   ☐ Strong, James. *Strong's Exhaustive Concordance of the Bible*. Abingdon Press, 1890. Entry G0172 (ἀκρατής).

   ☐ BibleHub Interlinear. "John 5:3 Greek Analysis." https://biblehub.com/interlinear/jo

hn/5-3.htm

3. **Impotency as a Poverty Cycle** — The concept of being "impotent" is extended to describe the poverty mindset: stuckness, lack of vision, delay due to fear, and the paralysis that occurs from waiting on external permission or perfect conditions.

☐ Payne, Tony. *The Poverty Mindset: Breaking Free from a Spirit of Lack*. Kingdom Builders Publishing, 2018.

☐ Maxwell, John C. *Failing Forward: Turning Mistakes into Stepping Stones for Success*. Thomas Nelson, 2000.

4. **Jim Rohn's Influence and Quote** — The quote "You are the average of the five people you spend the most time with" is a hallmark of Jim Rohn's philosophy on association and personal development.

☐ Rohn, Jim. *The Treasury of Quotes*. Brolin Publishing, 1994.

☐ Tracy, Brian. *Change Your Thinking, Change Your Life*. Wiley, 2003.

5. **Environmental Conditioning and Mental**

Normalization — The idea that we normalize dysfunction when surrounded by dysfunction is supported in both scripture and modern psychology. Social proximity and repeated exposure shape beliefs, motivation, and vision.

☐ Dweck, Carol S. *Mindset: The New Psychology of Success*. Random House, 2006.

☐ Cloud, Henry, and John Townsend. *Boundaries: When to Say Yes, How to Say No to Take Control of Your Life*. Zondervan, 1992.

Chapter 17

1. **Principle of Capacity Before Increase** — The idea that God often waits until we've made room—spiritually, mentally, and structurally—before He releases increase is seen throughout Scripture. Capacity and stewardship go hand in hand.

   ☐ Morris, Robert. *The Blessed Life: Unlocking the Rewards of Generous Living*. Bethany House, 2019.

   ☐ Evans, Tony. *Kingdom Stewardship: Managing All of Life Under God's Rule*. Focus on the Family,

2019.

2. **Growth Mindset in Business and Faith** — Coined by Carol Dweck, the growth mindset is the belief that abilities and potential can expand with effort, learning, and persistence. This psychological truth complements biblical faith principles about preparation and stewardship.
   ☐ Dweck, Carol S. *Mindset: The New Psychology of Success*. Random House, 2006.
   ☐ Maxwell, John C. *The 15 Invaluable Laws of Growth: Live Them and Reach Your Potential*. Center Street, 2012.

3. **Faith-Led Entrepreneurship** — The idea that faith involves planning and preparation before the manifestation of increase aligns with Christian entrepreneurial principles. You don't wait for growth to prepare—you prepare to grow.
   ☐ Green, Kenneth. *God's Plans for Your Success: A Guide to Understanding and Following God's Blueprint for Prosperity*. Charisma House, 2009.
   ☐ Stanley, Andy. *Visioneering: God's Blueprint for Developing and Maintaining Vision*. Multnomah Books, 2001.

Chapter 18

1. **Qavah" ()**חוקק – This Hebrew word is often translated as "wait" or "hope" in English. It conveys a deep sense of expectancy, to look eagerly for, or to bind together (perhaps by twisting). It appears in verses such as **Isaiah 40:31**, where it says, *"But those who wait (qavah) on the Lord shall renew their strength..."* (NLT: "trust in the Lord"). The word implies not passive waiting, but an active, hopeful anticipation of God's movement.

Referenced from:
Bible Hub Lexicon for Qavah (H6960). Retrieved from https://biblehub.com/hebrew/6960.htm

Chapter 19

1. **Dean Graziosi – "12 Keys to Business Success"** — Dean Graziosi is a renowned entrepreneur and author who teaches about strategic business growth. His analogy of mentorship as a "roadmap" emphasizes the value of learning from those ahead of you on the journey.
   ▫ Graziosi, Dean. *Millionaire Success Habits: The*

Gateway to Wealth and Prosperity. Hay House, 2016.

☐ Graziosi, Dean. *The Underdog Advantage: Rewrite Your Future by Turning Your Disadvantages into Superpowers*. Hay House, 2019.

☐ Graziosi, Dean. "12 Keys to Business Success." Live Event, 2024.

2. **Elijah and Elisha – The Mentorship Blueprint** — The relationship between Elijah and Elisha found in 1 Kings 19 and 2 Kings 2 serves as a foundational biblical example of mentorship. Elijah was instructed by God to anoint Elisha, who would eventually carry a double portion of his prophetic anointing.

    ☐ *The Holy Bible*. New Living Translation, Tyndale House Publishers, 2015. 1 Kings 19:19–21; 2 Kings 2:1–15.

    ☐ BibleGateway. "1 Kings 19; 2 Kings 2 (NLT)." https://www.biblegateway.com

3. **Mentorship as Acceleration** — The idea that mentorship accelerates progress is supported both in Scripture and business. Walking with someone who's been where you're going reduces guesswork and increases impact.

☐ Sinek, Simon. *Leaders Eat Last: Why Some Teams Pull Together and Others Don't*. Portfolio, 2014.

  ☐ Groeschel, Craig. *Lead Like It Matters: 7 Leadership Principles for a Church That Lasts*. Zondervan, 2022.

Chapter 20

1. **Biblical Example – The Apostle Paul** — Paul's life is a testimony of mission-driven endurance. He experienced extreme adversity, but his unwavering vision to spread the gospel gave him supernatural resolve.

   ☐ *The Holy Bible*. New Living Translation, Tyndale House Publishers, 2015. 2 Corinthians 11:23–27; Acts 20:24; Philippians 3:13–14.

   ☐ Bible Hub. "2 Corinthians 11 – Paul's Trials." https://biblehub.com

2. **Historical Example – Thomas Edison** — Edison's invention of the lightbulb came after thousands of failed experiments. His determination is a popular illustration of vision overcoming failure.

☐ Baldwin, Neil. *Edison: Inventing the Century*. Hyperion, 2001.

☐ "I have not failed. I've just found 10,000 ways that won't work." — Thomas Edison (attributed quote).

3. **Historical Example – Madam C.J. Walker (Sarah Breedlove)** — Faced with racial, gender, and financial adversity, she built a beauty empire that empowered African American women. She became the first documented female self-made millionaire in the U.S.

☐ Bundles, A'Lelia. *On Her Own Ground: The Life and Times of Madam C.J. Walker*. Scribner, 2001.

☐ National Women's History Museum. "Madam C.J. Walker." https://www.womenshistory.org

Chapter 21

Zōē Aiōnios – Abundant, Eternal Life

Strong's Exhaustive Concordance of the BibleZōē
  https://biblehub.com/greek/john/10-10.htm
Vine's Complete Expository Dictionary of Old and New Testament Words

— In John 10:10, Jesus promises more than mere survival; He offers Zōē life: real, active, and overflowing. This kind of life touches every domain—spiritual, mental, emotional, financial.

☐ Strong, James.

. Entry G2222 –

(ζωή): "life; both physical and spiritual, present and eternal."

☐ Bible Hub. "John 10:10 – Greek Analysis."

☐ Vine, W.E.

. Thomas Nelson, 1996.

Chapter 22

Chapter 23

DeMarco, MJ.

The Millionaire Fastlane: Crack the Code to Wealth and Live Rich for a Lifetime!

Viperion Publishing, 2011.

– This book explores the concept of creating scalable systems that generate income independently of time, shifting away from the traditional "slow lane" approach of working for wages.

What is CRM (Customer Relationship Management)?

See: Salesforce. "What is CRM?" https://www.salesforce.com/crm/

– CRM is a strategy and system used to manage a company's interactions with current and potential customers, typically via software. It automates tasks and synchronizes functions such as sales, marketing, and customer service to improve business relationships and growth.

(accessed April 2025).

Human Resources (HR) Defined

See: Society for Human Resource Management (SHRM). "What is Human Resources?" https://www.shrm.org/resourcesandtools/hr-topics/pages/default.aspx

– In business, Human Resources (HR) is responsible for managing the employee life cycle—including hiring, onboarding, training, performance management, compliance with labor laws, and separation. HR plays a key role in maintaining organizational culture, aligning personnel with the company's values and mission.

(accessed April 2025).

Modern Definition of Project Management

See: Project Management Institute (PMI). "What is Project Management?" https://www.pmi.org/about/learn-about-pmi/what-is-project-management

– Project management involves initiating, planning, executing, monitoring, and closing work to achieve specific goals within constraints such as time, cost, and resources. (accessed April 2025).

What is a Sales Funnel?

See: ClickFunnels. "What is a Sales Funnel?" https://www.clickfunnels.com/blog/what-is-a-sales-funnel/

– A sales funnel is a marketing model that represents the journey a prospect takes from becoming aware of a product or service to making a purchase. The funnel includes several stages, typically: Awareness, Interest, Consideration, Intent, Evaluation, and Purchase. The term "funnel" reflects the narrowing process—many enter at the top, but fewer convert at the bottom.

(accessed April 2025).

www.ingramcontent.com/pod-product-compliance
Lightning Source LLC
Chambersburg PA
CBHW031804220426
43662CB00007B/523